The Literacy Kit

IMAGINE, EXPLORE, ENTERTAIN

Geoff Barton

OXFORD

OXFORD
UNIVERSITY PRESS

Great Clarendon Street, Oxford OX2 6DP

Oxford University Press is a department of the University of Oxford.

It furthers the University's objective of excellence in research, scholarship, and education by publishing worldwide in

Oxford New York

Auckland Bangkok Buenos Aires Cape Town Chennai
Dar es Salaam Delhi Hong Kong Istanbul Karachi Kolkata
Kuala Lumpur Madrid Melbourne Mexico City Mumbai Nairobi
São Paulo Shanghai Taipei Tokyo Toronto

Oxford is a registered trade mark of Oxford University Press

in the UK and in certain other countries

© Geoff Barton 2001

First published 2001

The moral rights of the author have been asserted

Database right Oxford University Press (maker)

ACKNOWLEDGEMENTS

We are grateful for permission to reprint the following copyright material:

'Grandma Meets the Axe Murderer' by Diane Elliott and 'Moment of Decision' by Tina Milburn from *The World's Shortest Stories* edited by Steve Moss (Running Press, 1995), copyright © 1998, 1995 by Steve Moss, reprinted by permission of Running Press Book Publishers, Philadelphia and London, www.runningpress.com.

Joan Aiken: extract from 'Something' in *A Fit of Shivers* (Victor Gollancz, 1990), copyright © Joan Aiken Enterprises Ltd 1990, reprinted by permission of A. M. Heath & Co Ltd on behalf of Joan Aiken.

Enid Blyton: extract from *Five on Finniston Farm* (Hodder & Stoughton, 1960), reprinted by permission of Enid Blyton Ltd.

Kevin Crossley-Holland: extract from 'Arthur the King' in *Tales from the Old World* (Orion Children's Books, 2000), reprinted by permission of the publisher.

Roald Dahl: extract from 'The Umbrella Man' in *More Tales of the Unexpected* (Michael Joseph, 1980), reprinted by permission of David Higham Associates.

Len Deighton: extract from 'Mission Control: Hannibal One' in *Declarations of War* (Jonathan Clowes, 1971), copyright © Len Deighton 1971, © 2001 Pluriform Publishing Company BV, reprinted by permission of Jonathan Clowes Ltd, London, on behalf of Pluriform Publishing Company BV.

Emily Dickinson: 'There's Been a Death' from *The Poems of Emily Dickinson*, edited by Thomas H. Johnson (The Belknap Press of Harvard University Press), copyright © 1951, 1955, 1979 by the President and Fellows of Harvard College, reprinted by permission of the publishers and Trustees of Amherst College.

David Edgar: extract from Act 1, scene 1 of *The Life and Adventures of Nicholas Nickleby* (Michael Imison Playwrights, 1982), reprinted by permission of Methuen.

Rosanne Flynn: 'The City People Meet Themselves' first published in *Wondercrump Poetry!* edited by Jennifer Curry (Red Fox, 1994), reprinted by permission of The Random House Group Ltd.

Seamus Heaney: 'Mid-Term Break' from *Death of a Naturalist* (1966), reprinted by permission of the publishers, Faber & Faber Ltd.

Susan Hill: extract from *The Mist in the Mirror* (Vintage), copyright © Susan Hill 1992, reprinted by permission of Sheil Land Associates Ltd on behalf of the author.

Ted Hughes: 'The Warm and the Cold' from *Season Songs* (1976), reprinted by permission of the publishers, Faber & Faber Ltd.

Andy Martin: extract from *Walking on Water* (John Murray, 1995), reprinted by permission of David Higham Associates.

Michael Meyer (translator): extract from Act 1, Scene 1 of Henrik Ibsen: *An Enemy of the People* (Methuen, 1974), reprinted by permission of the publisher.

Edna St Vincent Millay: 'What lips my lips have kissed' from *Collected Poems* (HarperCollins), copyright © 1923, 1951 by Edna St Vincent Millay and Norma Millay Ellis, reprinted by permission of Elizabeth Barnett, Literary Executor. All rights reserved.

Arthur Miller (translator): extract from Act 1, Scene 1 of Henrik Ibsen: *An Enemy of the People* (Nick Hern Books, 1989), reprinted by permission of the publisher.

Brian Patten: 'Simple Lyric' from *Love Poems* (George Allen & Unwin, 1981), copyright © Brian Patten 1981, reprinted by permission of the author c/o Rogers, Coleridge & White Ltd, 20 Powis Mews, London W11 1JN

E. Annie Proulx: extract from *The Shipping News* (Fourth Estate, 1993), reprinted by permission of HarperCollins Publishers Ltd.

Henry Reed: 'Naming of Parts' from *Collected Poems* edited by Jon Stallworthy (OUP, 1991), reprinted by permission of Oxford University Press.

J. K. Rowling: extract from *Harry Potter and the Chamber of Secrets* (Bloomsbury, 1998), copyright © J. K. Rowling 1998, reprinted by permission of Christopher Little Literary Agency on behalf of the author.

We have tried to trace and contact all copyright holders before publication. If notified the publishers will be pleased to rectify any errors or omissions at the earliest opportunity.

We are grateful to the following for permission to reproduce photographs:

Mark Mason Studios (cover); Camera Press, p54; John Cleare Mountain Camera, p30; Mary Evans Picture Library, pp 78, 83, 107, 117; Eye Ubiquitous, p27; Ronald Grant Archive, pp 40-41, 43, 64; Frank Lane Picture Agency, p58; Moviestore Collection, p127; Photostage/Donald Cooper, pp 88-90; Popperfoto, pp 48-9, 61; Rex Features, pp 8, 110; Topham Picturepoint, pp 16, 21, 112; Universal Pictorial Press, p13

Other photographs by Alex Hibbs

The cartoon illustrations are by David Semple. Ilustrations on page 98 are by Richard Morris and page 99 are by Martin Aston

A CIP catalogue record for this book is available from the British Library.

ISBN 0 19 832036 1

10 9 8 7 6 5 4 3

Printed in Spain by Graficas Estella SA.

Orders and enquiries to Customer Services:

Tel: 01536 741068 **Fax:** 01536 454519

Contents

Introduction

Imagine, Explore, Entertain is a central part of *The Literacy Kit*. It provides the core texts you will need for developing pupils' reading, writing and spoken work.

You may have used one of the starter activities in the **Lesson Starters** boxes to kick the lesson off, and **OHTs** from the relevant pack to initiate whole-class discussion of text types and their features. Now comes the developmental stage, in which students focus on the specific word-, sentence- and text-level objectives of the *Framework for Teaching English 11–14*.

This Students' Book provides you with texts that are closely mapped to all the objectives and organized on a year-by-year basis, enabling you to plan more carefully and to ensure that essential text types and features are covered in each year. The **Objectives** box at the head of each text extract details the objectives addressed.

The texts always begin with an **Introduction**. This is a brisk, context-setting starter which tunes pupils into the text features they are looking at. It will get them focusing on the types of language and issues they can expect to be dealing with. You may want to develop this, asking pupils to make predictions before they start to read the text.

The **texts** themselves have been carefully selected to highlight some key features of structure and language, and to match the appropriate levels of interest and ability of pupils in different year groups. You'll find plenty of texts on contemporary subjects that should appeal to boys and girls aged 11–14.

The questions which follow provide for two levels of response. **Understanding the text** asks straightforward, fact-spotting questions. Don't underestimate the importance of these: they are the questions that quickly build pupils' confidence in skimming and scanning, helping them to identify key points quickly.

Interpreting the text offers more open-ended questions. Here pupils will need to give more reflective responses, often writing short paragraphs explaining and justifying their thoughts.

The **Language and structure** section highlights the new emphasis on language skills within the Framework. These are not arid, 'spot the split infinitive' style questions. Their focus is on language in use, getting pupils looking at writers' language decisions, cataloguing features of the text and then commenting on effect. This is the central part of the literacy process – emphasizing effect, and not simply spotting language features.

The **Writing activity** focuses on an aspect of the text and gets pupils responding in writing in a more developed way. They may be asked to practise a language skill in greater detail, or to rewrite part of the text in a different style. Importantly, this is the part of the process that shifts the emphasis from reading to writing. Having explored features of the writer's approach in a text, pupils now begin to write for themselves. It is part of the process of scaffolding writing.

Each unit concludes with an **Extended writing** task. Here the emphasis on developing pupils' writing skills is consolidated. These are bigger, more ambitious tasks which link back to the texts that pupils have been exploring. The tasks are scaffolded with suggestions, hints and, often, starter sentences. This approach should help pupils in the transition from dependent to independent writers.

Speaking and listening is integral to all English work and we know that you will be talking to students about their perceptions of texts throughout the process. We have also built in specific speaking and listening tasks where they develop language skills, or provide an opportunity to meet one of the *Framework* objectives.

In the **Teacher's Book** you will find a wealth of related resources, and the **OHT** pack provides those all-important acetates for a shared, whole-class focus on texts.

The Literacy Kit is, as you can see, a completely integrated scheme. I've been using it with my students here in Suffolk and the response to the variety, the rapid pace, and the sheer range of materials has been terrific – even from my more reluctant pupils!

I hope it proves similarly enjoyable and useful for you, helping you with the planning and delivery of the *Framework* in a lively and systematic way. Most of all, I hope your students have fun with the huge variety of new resources here.

Your feedback, via the website, would be very welcome.

Geoff Barton
www.oup.com/uk/litkit

Story openings

Introduction

Fiction writers often try to grab the reader's attention from the very start. They think of an arresting opening – something which makes us keen to read on – and then put twists and turns in the plot to keep our interest.

Many fiction texts use suspense to hold the reader's interest. We find this most in horror and ghost stories and in thrillers. To create suspense, the author gives hints and suggestions that a character faces danger, but keeps us waiting to see what happens.

This opening sequence from a horror story by Joan Aiken shows how one writer tries to capture and hold the reader's attention. The narrator is a young boy.

Something

Objectives

These are the objectives you will be studying:

- Word level: *word meaning in context*
- Sentence level: *starting paragraphs*, and *sentence variety*
- Reading: *character*, *setting and mood*, and *language choices* (how they enhance meanings)
- Writing: *story structure*, *characterization*, and *narrative devices* (using a range of devices to involve the reader)

Glossary

fusillade – *volley of shots, like lots of guns being fired at once*

gentian – *small flower*

Something

When the thing happened for the first time I was digging up wild lilies to plant in my own little garden. Digging up wild lilies. A happy task. They are dark orange and grow down by the narrow shallow brook that freezes solid in winter. On that day it was babbling and murmuring placidly and I sang a song, which I made up as I went along, to keep company with its murmur. 'Wild lilies I find, wild lilies I bring, wild lilies, wild lilies, to flower in the spring.' Overhead the alder trees arched, and water-birds, becoming used to my harmless presence, called their short gargling answers. Once or twice a kingfisher flashed. There were trout in the water, but only tiny ones; I could feel them brush against my bare legs every now and then as I waded knee-deep along the course of the brook, which made an easier route than the tangled banks.

At the end of a whole afternoon spent in this manner my mind felt bare, washed clean, like the stones in the brook.

And then – suddenly: fear. Where did it come from? I had no means of knowing. *Menace*. Cold fear was all around me – in the dark arch of the trees, the tunnel they made (into which the stream vanished), the sharp croak of birds, the icy grip of the water on my calves, the gritty scour of mud on my grimed and scraped hands. But, most of all, in my own mind, as if, down at the back of it, stood something hidden, watchful, *waiting*. In another minute I would *see* it and know what it was. In another minute I would go mad from terror.

Frenzied with haste to be away from there I scrambled up the bank, snatching my trowel and the wooden bucket in which I had been putting my lily roots – dropping half of

them; panic-stricken, never looking back, I thrust and battered a track through alders and brambles, tearing my shirt, scratching my arms and face. Mother would be furious, but I never gave that a thought. All my need was to get home – home – home to Grandfather's comforting presence.

Barefoot I ran over the ploughed field, stubbing my toes on flints, reckless of sharp stubble-ends and dry thistles with their lancing spines. Tonight I would need to spend hours squeezing them out, painfully one by one. Tonight was not now. Now if I did not find Grandfather I would die of fear.

Luckily he was always to be found in the same place: placid on a backless chair with his dog Flag beside him, outside the smithy where my uncles Josef and Willi clanked on the anvil and roared on the bellows. A great grey cart-horse waited patiently, one hoof tipped forward. A cone of fire burned bright in the dim forge, and there was Uncle Josef in his black leather apron, holding the gold and blazing shoe in his long tongs. For once I didn't wait and watch. I ran and clung tight to Grandfather. He felt frail and bony, and smelt, as always, of straw and old-man's-odour, and sweet tobacco.

'Grandfather – Grandfather – ' I gulped.

Holding me in thin strong hands he looked at me long and shrewdly with his faded shrunken eyes.

'So it's happened, has it?'

'Yes. Yes. It has. But what *is* it, Grandfather? *What* has happened?'

'Easy. Easy!' He soothed me with his voice as if I had been a panicky foal. 'It was bound to come. It always does. Your father – your brothers – now you. All our family. It always happens, sooner or later.'

'But what? But what?'

A terrific fusillade of clangs came from the forge. Uncle Josef had the shoe back on the anvil and was reshaping it with powerful blows of his hammer. A fan of sparks rained out, making the cart-horse stamp and whinny.

'Come along,' said my grandfather. 'We'll walk to the church.' He put his hand on my shoulder to hoist himself into a walking position, then kept it there, for balance. He was very stooped, and walked with a limp; still, for his years, he was as strong as an old root.

We went slowly along the village street. Marigolds blazed, nasturtiums climbed up the sides of the ancient timbered houses. Apples on the trees were almost ripe. The sky, though cloudless and blue as a gentian, was covered with a light haze; in the mornings and evenings now, mist lay thick in the valley. It was September.

'Winter is coming,' said my grandfather.

'Yes, Grandfather.'

'Winter is a kind of night,' he said. 'For months we are prisoners here in the village. As, at night, we are shut in our homes. The next village is a world's end away.'

It was true. Our village lies in a deep valley. Often in winter the roads are blocked with snow for weeks, sometimes for months. Up to now I had never minded this. It was good fun, being closed away from the world. We had huge stacks of firewood – cellars full of wine and flour. The cows and sheep were stabled safely. We had dried fruits, stored apples, fiddles, music, jokes, and a few books. We had each other. What more did we need? Up to now I had loved the winter. But at this moment I shivered, as I pictured miles of gale-scoured hills, the snow sent by wind into long curving drifts, with never a human footprint. Darkness over the mountains for thirteen hours, from sunset to sunrise.

'Night is a kind of death,' said my grandfather. And then: 'You know that I have bad dreams.'

Indeed I *did*. His yells when he woke from one of those legendary dreams were terrible to hear; they almost made the blood run backwards in your veins. Yet he would never tell us what the dreams had been about; he would sit (once he was awake) white, panting, shaking, gasping, by his bed; sometimes he might have hurled himself right out of his cot, an arm's length away from it, and, next day, would be covered in black bruises, and his eyes sunken in deep grey hollows.

Joan Aiken

UNDERSTANDING THE TEXT

1 The first paragraph sets the scene. Where does the story take place?

2 What time of day is it?

3 In paragraph three the narrator feels fear. What is it that is frightening him?

4 Why does he decide to run to his grandfather's house?

5 What is surprising about the grandfather's reaction when the narrator arrives at his house?

INTERPRETING THE TEXT

6 A good horror story will create a feeling of suspense. How does the title of this story begin to do this?

7 Look more closely at the first paragraph. Compare the first sentence with the rest of the paragraph. How does the writer gain and then hold the reader's interest here?

8 What do we learn from the story about the character of the boy who narrates the story? Look at how he is presented by the writer:

   ◆ what he does

   ◆ his relationship with his grandfather.

   Try to find three key points about the boy's character.

9 What do you learn from the story about the place where the boy lives? Does it feel similar to or different from your own environment?

10 Story writers have to put across moods strongly. How does the writer make the grandfather's dreams seem so chilling?

11 At the beginning of the story, it is not clear *when* the events are set. But hints build up about this through the extract. Find four clues that the story is set in the past.

LANGUAGE AND STRUCTURE

1 Look more closely at how the author uses language to build suspense.

The writer structures the start of her story like this:

Paragraph 1: focus on the setting (except for the first sentence)
Paragraph 2: the narrator feels calm
Paragraph 3: the narrator feels sudden fear
Paragraph 4: the narrator begins to run

a Why do you think after the first sentence the writer has two paragraphs in which everything seems 'normal'?

b Look at paragraph 3: how does it seem different in style from the two paragraphs before it?

> **HINT**
>
> ● Look at the types of sentences, their length and structure

c Look at the verbs used in paragraph 4: *scrambled, snatching, dropping, thrust, tearing, scratching.* What have these verbs got in common, and why do you think the writer uses them?

2 Look at the second half of the story. It uses many abstract nouns, such as *winter, night, darkness, dreams.* But in the last paragraph the tone is much more urgent and the vocabulary more immediate: *blood, veins, panting, shaking, gasping, hurled, bruises.*

How does all of this build up the sense of suspense? Start your answer like this:

a The abstract nouns (*winter, night, darkness, dreams*) create a feeling of …

b The last paragraph is very different. It …

3 Horror writers often hold back information to keep us reading. How does this writer do so? What kinds of questions were you asking as you read the story?

   a Write down two questions which might be in a reader's mind at the end of the first paragraph.

   b Write down two questions that the reader might ask at the end of the extract.

Questions might start like this:

◆ Why did the boy …?

◆ Where does …?

◆ Why was the grandfather …?

WRITING ACTIVITY

The story is told in a first-person style. The writer tells the story using pronouns like *I* and *me*. It would be possible to re-tell the story in a number of other styles:

A **third-person** style would tell the story using *he* and *they*.

Example: *When the thing happened for the first time he was digging up wild lilies to plant in his own little garden.*

A **second person**-style would tell it using the pronoun *you*.

Example: *When the thing happened for the first time you were digging up wild lilies to plant in your own little garden.*

The story could also be retold using a different form – as a letter (from the boy to the grandfather, or the grandfather to the boy) looking back on the events; as a diary entry; or as a spoken story, retold by the boy or the grandfather one evening much later.

Experiment with rewriting the story using a different point of view (second- or third-person), and a different form. Write a paragraph or two, changing the original style, but keeping the same basic storyline.

Write a few sentences to describe how your rewritten version creates a different effect.

Plots, crises, and resolutions

Introduction

These texts are two very short stories. Because they are complete, you can study in miniature the way that stories open, develop and end.

Two Very Short Stories

OBJECTIVES

You will be studying the following objectives:

- Word level: *word meaning in context*
- Reading: *infer and deduce* (understand implied meanings from evidence in the text), *character, setting and mood, language choices* (how they enhance meanings), and *endings*
- Writing: *story structure*, and *narrative devices* (using a range of devices to involve the reader)

GLOSSARY

booty – *treasure*

Text A

Grandma Meets the Axe Murderer

The crazed axe-murderer approached the house. Having ravaged the entire neighbourhood, his sack of booty was almost full.

Alone inside, the old woman sat knitting. The murderer raised his blood-stained axe and rang the porch doorbell.

Slowly, she opened the door and peered into his face.

'Trick or treat!' the little boy shouted.

Diane Elliott

Text B

Moment of Decision

She could almost hear the prison door clanging shut.

Freedom would be gone forever, control of her own destiny gone, never to return.

Wild thoughts of flight flashed through her mind. She knew there was no escape.

She turned to the groom with a smile and repeated the words, 'I do.'

Tina Milburn

UNDERSTANDING THE TEXT

Text A

1 Sum up the story in a sentence.

2 How does the writer make the 'axe murderer' seem menacing?

3 How does she make the old woman seem like an innocent victim?

Text B

4 Why do you think the text is called 'Moment of Decision'?

5 Where did you think the story was set until the last sentence? Where is it actually set?

INTERPRETING THE TEXT

6 Both stories avoid using names for the characters. Why do you think this is?

7 Choose the story you like most, and answer the following questions:

- What did the title lead you to expect?
- What was your first impression of what the story was about?
- When did you spot the twist in the tale?

8 Which story is least successful in your opinion? Try to say why.

> ## HINT
>
> - To give a well-developed answer, refer specifically to the texts. Use examples in quotation marks to support your comments.

LANGUAGE AND STRUCTURE

1 The stories follow a similar structure to many short stories. They both build up our expectations and then surprise us with a twist at the end. Use a table like this to show how the structure of the two stories works:

What the first section makes us expect	How the last sentence surprises us
Text A:	
Text B:	

2 The 'twist' in each story changes how the reader understands what has gone before. Look at the second sentence in text A.

   a What does it mean when you first read it?

   b What does it mean when you have read the whole story?

3 Text B creates tension by using only the pronoun 'she'.

   a How does using 'she' build tension?

   b What might the writer have said instead of using a pronoun in this way?

4 Both stories use dramatic vocabulary – words like *crazed, ravaged, blood-stained, clanging, destiny, wild.*

   a Take text A and retell it using less dramatic words.

   b Say whether the story now has less tension, and why.

WRITING ACTIVITY

Write a 55-word short story which follows the same pattern as these two. Make the reader imagine one storyline, then challenge him or her with a very different ending. Your story might start:

◆ like a love story

◆ as a thriller

◆ like a letter.

UNIT 1

EXTENDED WRITING

Choose one of the very short stories on page 7 and make it into the opening of a radio script. Your aim is to grab the attention of the listener through a piece of radio drama. This means that you will need:

◆ dialogue between characters

◆ sound effects to help set the scene.

You might start with dialogue, or a sound effect, or you might use a narrator to introduce the storyline.

Here is an example of how you could start your rewritten version of text A, 'Grandma Meets the Axe Murderer'.

Sound effect: *wind howling*

Sound effect: *footsteps outside*

Sound effect: *sudden silence. Sound of knitting needles.*

Sound effect: *woman gently humming*

Old woman: What a night. Listen to that wind …

Once you have devised your script, spend time in pairs or a small group rehearsing a performance of it, either for your class or to record on tape.

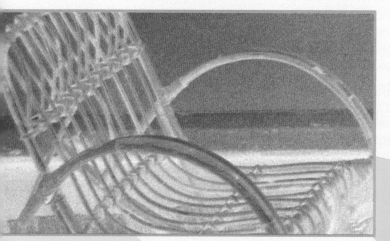

Description, dialogue, and action

Introduction

Novels and short stories tell us tales about characters, often with a focus on just one or two central characters whom we follow through the storyline. The main character of a story is called the **protagonist**.

Writers can tell us about characters in different ways. They might use **description**:

Harry Potter was not a normal boy …

or **action**:

Harry's scar began to hurt …

or **dialogue**:

Harry thought for a moment. 'You can't be serious,' he said …

This unit looks at an extract from *Harry Potter and the Chamber of Secrets* to explore the way characters are presented. Harry Potter and his friends Hermione and Ron are excited to be joining the school duelling club. Their hearts sink, however, when they learn that the class will be led by the big-headed smoothie, Gilderoy Lockhart. He plans to demonstrate duelling, assisted by the unpleasant Professor Snape.

Harry Potter and the Duelling Club

OBJECTIVES

You will be studying the following objectives:

- Word level: *unfamiliar words* (working out their meaning), and *words in different languages*

- Sentence level: *subordinate clauses, noun phrases,* and *speech punctuation*

- Reading: *infer and deduce* (understand implied meanings from evidence in the text), *character, setting and mood,* and *language choices* (how they enhance meanings)

- Writing: *characterization,* and *link writing and reading* (make links between your reading and your choices as a writer)

- Speaking and listening: *collaborate on scripts*

GLOSSARY

Slytherins – *students who belong to one of the four school Houses, Slytherin*

Harry Potter and the Duelling Club

Snape's upper lip was curling. Harry wondered why Lockhart was still smiling; if Snape had been looking at *him* like that he'd have been running as fast as he could in the opposite direction.

Lockhart and Snape turned to face each other and bowed; at least, Lockhart did, with much twirling of his hands, whereas Snape jerked his head irritably. Then they raised their wands like swords in front of them.

'As you see, we are holding our wands in the accepted combative position,' Lockhart told the silent crowd. 'On the count of three, we will cast our first spells. Neither of us will be aiming to kill, of course.'

'I wouldn't bet on that,' Harry murmured, watching Snape baring his teeth.

'One – two – three –'

Both of them swung their wands up and over their shoulders. Snape cried '*Expelliarmus!*' There was a dazzling flash of scarlet light and Lockhart was blasted off his feet: he flew backwards off the stage, smashed into the wall and slid down it to sprawl on the floor.

Malfoy and some of the other Slytherins cheered. Hermione was dancing on tiptoes. 'Do you think he's all right?' she squealed through her fingers.

'Who cares?' said Harry and Ron together.

Lockhart was getting unsteadily to his feet. His hat had fallen off and his wavy hair was standing on end.

'Well, there you have it!' he said, tottering back onto the platform. 'That was a Disarming Charm – as you see, I've lost my wand – ah, thank you, Miss Brown. Yes, an excellent idea to show them that, Professor Snape, but if you don't mind my saying so, it was very obvious what you were about to do. If I had wanted to stop you it would have been only too easy. However, I felt it would be instructive to let them see ...'

Snape was looking murderous. Possibly Lockhart had noticed, because he said, 'Enough demonstrating! I'm going to come amongst you now and put you all into pairs. Professor Snape, if you'd like to help me ...'

They moved through the crowd, matching up partners. Lockhart teamed Neville with Justin Finch-Fletchley, but Snape reached Harry and Ron first.

'Time to split up the dream team, I think,' he sneered. 'Weasley, you can partner Finnigan. Potter –'

Harry moved automatically towards Hermione.

'I don't think so,' said Snape, smiling coldly. 'Mr Malfoy, come over here. Let's see what you make of the famous Potter. And you, Miss Granger – you can partner Miss Bulstrode.'

Malfoy strutted over, smirking. Behind him walked a Slytherin girl who reminded Harry of a picture he'd seen in *Holidays with Hags*. She was large and square and her heavy jaw jutted aggressively. Hermione gave her a weak smile which she did not return.

'Face your partners!' called Lockhart, back on the platform, 'and bow!'

Harry and Malfoy barely inclined their heads, not taking their eyes off each other.

'Wands at the ready!' shouted Lockhart. 'When I count to three, cast your charms to disarm your opponent – *only* to disarm them – we don't want

any accidents. One ... two ... three ...'

Harry swung his wand over his shoulder, but Malfoy had already started on 'two': his spell hit Harry so hard he felt as though he'd been hit over the head with a saucepan. He stumbled, but everything still seemed to be working, and wasting no more time, Harry pointed his wand straight at Malfoy and shouted, '*Rictusempra!*'

A jet of silver light hit Malfoy in the stomach and he doubled up, wheezing.

'*I said disarm only!*' Lockhart shouted in alarm over the heads of the battling crowd, as Malfoy sank to his knees; Harry had hit him with a Tickling Charm, and he could barely move for laughing. Harry hung back, with a vague feeling it would be unsporting to bewitch Malfoy while he was on the floor, but this was a mistake. Gasping for breath, Malfoy pointed his wand at Harry's knees, choked, '*Tarantallegra!*' and next second Harry's legs had begun to jerk around out of his control in a kind of quickstep.

'Stop! Stop!' screamed Lockhart, but Snape took charge.

'*Finite Incantatem!*' he shouted; Harry's feet stopped dancing, Malfoy stopped laughing and they were able to look up.

J. K. Rowling

UNDERSTANDING THE TEXT

1 How can you tell that Gilderoy Lockhart is, at first, very self-confident?

2 What hints are there that Professor Snape is not happy?

3 How can you tell that Harry and Ron do not like either teacher?

4 How does Malfoy cheat in the charm duelling?

5 What different types of spells do Harry Potter and Malfoy use during their duel?

INTERPRETING THE TEXT

6 How does the author show the reader that Snape is an unpleasant character?

7 Look more closely at the way Gilderoy Lockhart is presented in the extract. How does the writer make him a figure of fun? You might mention:

  ♦ the way he speaks

  ♦ what happens in his duel with Snape

  ♦ how he reacts to this.

8 How does the writer make the scene comic? Think about:

  ♦ descriptions of people

  ♦ use of dialogue

  ♦ events that take place.

LANGUAGE AND STRUCTURE

1 Look at what Gilderoy Lockhart says. In what ways is his language typical of teachers?

HINT

- Look at the way he speaks to the students
- Look for any typical 'teacher' words and phrases

2 Look at the names the writer uses:

Gilderoy Lockhart
Harry Potter
Ron Weasley
Professor Snape
Malfoy
Justin Finch-Fletchley

Some of these names sound comic. Some sound menacing.
Some seem fairly neutral.

a Group them into the three categories – comic, menacing and neutral.

b Choose one of the names and try to describe how it achieves its effect – how it sounds either comic, menacing or neutral.

3 Look at the language of the charms:

Expelliarmus
Rictusempra
Tarantallegra
Finite Incantatem

a Using the context of the story, write down a definition for what you think each command means.

b Are there any clues in the spelling of the words about what they might mean? Do they remind you of words in another language?

4   Occasionally, to add detail, writers use subordinate clauses to expand noun phrases – like this:

a Slytherin girl **who reminded Harry of a picture he'd seen in Holidays with Hags**

Hermione gave her a weak smile **which she did not return**

For each of the noun phrases below, think of a subordinate clause which would expand it to add detail:

a   Lockhart and Snape, who …, turned to face each other.

b   On the count of three we will cast our first spells, which …

c   Harry's feet, which …, stopped dancing.

5   Look at the way the writer integrates speech into larger sentences.

a   She uses punctuation to show where the speech begins and ends. Write down one of these sentences and label the punctuation, saying what each item is and what it tells you.

b   She finds alternatives for the speech verb 'said'. Write down three other words she uses.

c   Sometimes the speech verb is placed *before* the spoken words, like this:

Possibly Lockhart had noticed, because he said, 'Enough demonstrating!'

Sometimes it is placed *after* the spoken words:

'I don't think so,' said Snape, smiling coldly.

Write down one more example of the writer integrating speech into longer sentences.

WRITING ACTIVITY

As we have seen, novelists can use plot, description and dialogue to show their characters. What about dramatists and screenplay writers? They really only have characters' dialogue available.

Look at this moment from the novel. How would you show it in a screenplay or drama text?

Snape's upper lip was curling. Harry wondered why Lockhart was still smiling; if Snape had been looking at him like that he'd have been running as fast as he could in the opposite direction.

Lockhart and Snape turned to face each other and bowed; at least, Lockhart did, with much twirling of his hands, whereas Snape jerked his head irritably. They raised their wands like swords in front of them.

You might consider:

◆ using a narrator's voice (e.g. Harry or Ron) to describe what they see

◆ getting the characters to talk or think aloud

◆ using another witness to describe the scene.

You might start like this:

> **Harry:** Look at the way Snape's lip's curling!
>
> **Ron:** Yeah, he looks furious. Makes you wonder why Lockhart's still able to smile …

Working in pairs, have a go at writing this section as a script.

1 First, discuss how you will approach the task, and then develop a draft.

2 Compare your draft with that of other people in your group.

3 Choose one of the scripts written by the group, and compare it in detail with the original version given above. Does it use many of the same words?

EXTENDED WRITING

J. K. Rowling presents characters by using different methods. She uses description, plot and dialogue. Practise doing this yourself. Take the character notes below and write the opening sequence of a story which shows what that character is like.

Character summary:

Celia Merchant

- ◆ New English teacher
- ◆ 40s, small, speaks quickly
- ◆ eyes wrinkle when she smiles
- ◆ has high standards, is impatient when things don't get done.

Setting:

School corridor, first day of term

Plot:

She sees two pupils arguing and decides to find out what is happening

Story openings

You could start with one of these story-openings.

Description:

The corridor was crowded and the new teacher emerged from Room 23. She was …

Plot:

Celia Merchant heard the argument before she saw it. She moved quickly out of room 23 …

Dialogue:

'All right,' came a voice, 'that's enough. Break it up.'

Choose one of the story-openings above and write the rest of the paragraph. Try to show all the different features listed in the character summary.

Involving the reader

Introduction

Writers aim to get the reader as involved in their stories as possible. They use a range of techniques, including:

- telling the story from different points of view (e.g. using the first, second or third person)

- using a different time sequence (e.g. starting with a crime, and then using flashbacks to show what led to it)

- using more than one narrative (e.g. telling the interlocking stories of two characters)

- experimenting with tense (e.g. suddenly shifting into the present tense)

- deliberately confusing the reader (e.g. not telling us the name of a character, to keep us wondering who it is).

This extract is from Susan Hill's ghost story, *The Mist in the Mirror*.

Finding his way in darkness to his room in an inn, the narrator is about to encounter a strange supernatural presence. Notice how Susan Hill builds a sense of panic and mystery. Use the questions which follow to explore the techniques she uses to keep the reader involved.

The Mist in the Mirror

OBJECTIVES

You will be studying the following objectives:

- Sentence level: *tense management*

- Reading: *character, setting and mood*, and *language choices* (how they enhance meanings)

- Writing: *narrative devices* (using a range of devices to involve the reader)

The Mist in the Mirror

GLOSSARY

traverse – *move across*

flailing – *thrashing about (trying to regain balance)*

skeins – *loosely coiled threads*

peremptory – *commanding, bossy*

crone – *old person*

The Mist in the Mirror

The Inn was in darkness. I barred the front door, shot the iron bolts and then felt my way across the hall, groping with my hand outstretched for the stair rail, for there was no window through which the moonlight could penetrate, and no lamp or torch had been left out for me. I thought that by now I knew my way to the upper floors and my own room but at the second landing must have taken a wrong turning, for up here was a warren of short, narrow passageways leading out of one another, and, finding only a blank wall immediately ahead of me, I backed a few yards, before moving cautiously on again. I edged forwards step by step putting my hand out again to keep in contact with the wall on my left. I was afraid of pressing the latch of the wrong door and entering a strange room, uncertain whether to call out, though quite sure that the morose landlord would not thank me for disturbing him.

Then, at the end of the passage, I made out a dim, reddish glow, as if from the last embers of a fire, and began to move towards it, thinking that I might somehow get my bearings there, or at least recognise some familiar-looking corner.

The light did not increase greatly as I drew nearer but seemed to be oddly veiled or obscured. The distance along the corridor was only a few yards, and yet to traverse it took an eternity, I was so tired and dazed.

Then, abruptly, I came much closer to the source of the light, and at the same moment, missed my footing on the single step that was in my way. I reached out my arm, flailing, to save myself and just managed to do so, but I reeled nonetheless, and my hand touched not empty air, nor any solid wall or door but instead, to my horror, came up against and went straight through a screen or curtain made of beads that clung and trailed about me like skeins as I stumbled, so that I felt them not only on my hands and arms but about my head and face too. The sensation in the darkness was a horrible one, but worse was to follow.

Looking up I saw that the curtain did indeed cover an open doorway and that behind a small, dark inner lobby, at the entrance to which I was now standing, lay a room. I could make out little and my impression of it was swift and muddled, in my own confusion and the shock of almost falling. I saw a round table and, beside it though set back a little, a chair, in which sat an old woman. The glow came from a single dim lamp which stood on the table, its lights veiled by some kind of reddish-coloured cloth. The woman wore a scarf, tied gypsy-fashion about her forehead, and she seemed to be dressed in shawls of some dark flowing stuff. All of this I no more than glimpsed before she looked up and directly at me, though how much she could see of me in the dimness I do not know. But I saw her. I saw the black pits of her eyes with a pin-prick gleam at their centre, and a swarthiness and greasiness about her skin; I saw her hands laid on top of one another, old, scrawny, claw-like hands they seemed to me; and the flash of a spark from some jewelled or enamelled ring.

It has taken minutes to describe, and I break out in a sweat as I re-live the scene, and yet to see the picture of her there beyond the bead curtain in that dark, redly glowing room, took only seconds, but in those seconds it impressed itself upon my inner eye and my imagination and memory forever, and awoke some deep, fearful response within me.

I do not know whether I cried out, I only knew that I recoiled almost at the very instant of first feeling the curtain and seeing the old woman, and backed away, stumbling again, wrenching my hands from the wretched, clinging strands – I can still hear the soft slack noise of its falling off me and back upon itself as I fled. But in my haste I fell again, this time against a piece of furniture set back to the wall, and jarred myself badly and, through the noise and my own cursings, heard a peremptory voice and saw a light, as a door at the end of the passage was opened.

The landlord showed me the way back to my room, from which I had been only a few paces, with an ill grace, and I could not have blamed him for that, but in fact I was very little aware of his sullen complaints and remonstrations, I was so caught up within my own disorientation and fear.

I did not come to or calm myself until I had been alone for some time, sitting in the silence on my bed. I had been badly frightened, not by dark nor by losing my way of course, those were trivial matters, but by what I had seen, the old crone draped in her gypsy-like scarves and shawls, sitting at a table in a dark room before a veiled lamp. Yet rack my brains as I might I could think of nothing in the reality of that to terrify a grown man who had travelled alone to some of the remotest parts of the world and seen almost daily sights a thousand times more horrifying and strange. My heart had pounded and was still beating too fast, my mouth was dry, my brain seemed to burn and crackle with the over-alertness of a state of nervous dread. Yet why? I had to conclude that I was not frightened by what I had actually seen so much as by some memory it had stirred, or something that had terrified me long ago. I could recall nothing, though I beat at my brains for most of that night, for I did not sleep again until dawn. I only knew that, whenever I saw the old woman with my inner eye, I started back, wanting desperately to get away, avoid the sight of her face and figure, her look, and, above all, to avoid entering the darkened room that lay beyond the beaded curtain.

Susan Hill

UNDERSTANDING THE TEXT

1 How can you tell from the first paragraph that the inn is old?

2 At first, what does the narrator think the dim red light might be? Describe it in your own words.

3 In a sentence say what the old woman looks like.

4 The narrator reacts in shock at the sight. How does he then hurt himself?

5 What is the landlord's attitude as he helps the narrator?

6 Reflecting, why is the narrator so disturbed by what he saw?

INTERPRETING THE TEXT

7 Look more closely at paragraph 4 ('Then, abruptly …'). What different feelings and emotions does the narrator have here?

8 Look at the way the writer describes the old woman in paragraph 5. Her vocabulary helps us to visualize what the narrator sees. She also refers to other senses. Explore the writer's choice of words under the following headings:

   ◆ words suggesting colour, or lack of colour

   ◆ words suggesting texture

   ◆ words suggesting objects that are difficult to see exactly

   ◆ comparisons (one object compared to another)

   ◆ words that create a sense of mystery or horror

9 How does the writer build tension in the extract? Look for the way she:

   ◆ makes the setting mysterious

   ◆ uses powerful vocabulary to create a vivid atmosphere

   ◆ shows the fear the narrator feels

   ◆ hints at things that may happen later

   ◆ holds back information from the reader.

   Write a paragraph using some of these points, with examples.

LANGUAGE AND STRUCTURE

1 Is it possible to create tension without using description? Take paragraph 5 again, in which the narrator sees the old woman. Try rewriting this paragraph using as few descriptive words as possible. Make it seem much more like a factual report. This

means that you may wish to shorten sentences as well. For example, you might start like this:

I saw that the curtain covered a doorway with a room behind.

a Rewrite the rest of the paragraph.

b Now write a sentence or two describing how the new text feels different. Is there still the same feeling of emotion and tension?

2 The text is written in the first person ('I do not know …'). What would it be like in the second person ('You do not know …') or the third person ('He does not know …')?

Take paragraph 7 (beginning 'I do not know') and rewrite it using the second person for the first (long) sentence, and the third person for the rest of the paragraph.

Then write two sentences describing how the text feels different in each of the different modes.

3 Look at the start of paragraph 6. Susan Hill shifts into the present tense at this point:

It has taken minutes to describe, and I break out in a sweat as I re-live the scene …

Why do you think she changes the time sequence in this way? What effect does it have on us as we read the story?

WRITING ACTIVITY

Practise using techniques which hold the reader's attention.

The narrator is disturbed by the sight of the old woman. Imagine that on his way back to the inn one evening a week later, he wanders into an alleyway and catches another glimpse of the old woman, perhaps looking out from the window of a shop.

Aim for maximum tension. Start with the narrator walking, as normal, then turning into the alleyway. Show the evening getting darker. Show the narrator glancing into a shop window as he passes. Then describe what he sees and how he reacts.

Aim to write two or three paragraphs. Try to make your style similar to what you have seen in the text by Susan Hill.

EXTENDED WRITING

Take a well-known story, such as a fairy-tale or legend. Think about techniques you could use to tell that story so that the reader would be closely involved.

You might consider the following techniques, described at the beginning of this unit:

* different points of view
* different time sequences
* more than one narrative
* experimenting with tense
* deliberately confusing the reader.

Look at the story openers below, which are all telling the story of Little Red Riding Hood. Choose one as your own starting-point and then write the opening section (or all) of the story. Aim for maximum reader involvement.

Different point of view

I was late setting out that day. I got up late and I didn't feel well. It was after nine when I finally made my way into the forest. It was a bright, fresh morning and I was hungry. Then in the distance, through the glades, beyond the dell, I caught a glimpse of someone skipping, someone in red, someone who obviously hadn't been warned to stay on the forest path because I am dangerous ...

Different time sequence

'I don't know how I can ever thank you,' said Grandma, as she finished washing her face. She looked at me and held out her arms. The woodsman bowed slightly and stepped out of the cottage without saying a word. Hugging me now, Grandma became tearful. 'Imagine,' she said, 'just imagine what could have happened.'

It was three hours earlier that I had set off. The sun was shining and ...

More than one narrative

'I'm leaving,' I called to Mother as I stepped through the door.

'Stay on the path,' I heard her shout as I closed the latch behind me. Same every time. She was such a worrier.

Meanwhile the wolf was feeling irritable. He hadn't had a good morning so far …

Experimenting with tense

I remember that path so well. It will probably always stay in my memory. It winds through glades and copses, leads you into small dips, through shadows and bright patches, safe and reassuring, but also a little dull.

That morning I thought most about how dull the path was. It was then that I decided …

Deliberately confusing the reader

Something moved in the shadows. Then it stopped. It seemed to be watching, or at least listening.

I paused. A bird flew overhead breaking the silence. Something rattled in the tops of the trees.

I felt my heart beating faster. Flap. That bird again. Flap, flap. I moved on.

Once you have written your story sequence, write a one-paragraph commentary describing some of the techniques you have used. Say whether you feel you have been successful in achieving the effects you aimed for.

Using imagery

Introduction

Writers of fiction and poetry often create special language effects. They might use images to help us visualize a scene more clearly – for example, 'the sea swelled like a monster stirring'. They might use patterns of sound – for example, 'I **f**ound the **f**ear I **f**elt I'd lost'. Poets in particular will use a range of language devices, such as rhythm and rhyme.

We call all of this figurative language. It's worth remembering that many types of texts use figurative language - not only stories and poems. For example, you will find alliteration in newspaper headlines and in adverts. Non-fiction writers may use imagery to make essays, articles and speeches more vivid. But in poetry we can often find figurative language used in its most concentrated form.

This unit looks at figurative language in two poems, a descriptive poem written in the 20th century, and a ballad (a poem telling a story) from the 18th century.

City and Country

OBJECTIVES

You will be studying the following objectives:

- Word level: *word meaning in context*, *unfamiliar words* (working out their meaning), and *connectives*
- Sentence level: *sentences in older text*
- Reading: *character*, *setting and mood*, *language choices* (how they enhance meanings), and *poetic form*
- Writing: *visual and sound effects*, and *evocative description*

Text A

This poem by Rosanne Flynn describes a scene rather than telling a story. It is about the commuters and other travellers on a train, and the relationship they have with each other.

> ### GLOSSARY
> **aura** – *surrounding glow*

The City People Meet Themselves

The city people meet themselves
as they stare in the mirror of the opposite seat.
An old woman smiles at her reflection –
a girl, who's late for work
and urges the train on with a tapping foot –
the crumpled old woman remembers when
her feet tapped to speed up life
but now the feet are tired and old
and each step aches with dwindling hours:
a starched commuter tries not to look
at the broken-down man who cries –
his shallow eyes, pools of hopelessness,
the business man prays that life will be kind
and the treadmill of time will not leave him to cry
in the loneliness of a busy train;
an eager boy gapes at his reflection,
a huge man whose long arms reach to the straps
and smothers the boy in an aura of greatness –
the boy longs for the distant time
when his arms will reach
into the unknown realms of adulthood;
a worn out mother stares across
and sees another woman with the same gaze
grateful for child, but mournful for freedom.
Their eyes meet in silent conversation.

Rosanne Flynn

27

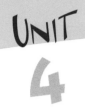

UNIT 4

Text B

This poem from the 18th century recounts a legend from North Wales. It is about Llewelyn, a man who goes out hunting, only to find on his return that his faithful dog, Gelert, appears to have murdered his only child.

Ballads are an important tradition in poetry. They use verse to tell stories, often using rhythm and rhyme to create a strong feeling of spoken language – originally, ballads were intended to be spoken aloud.

> ### GLOSSARY
>
> **brach** – *female hound*
>
> **board** – *table*
>
> **sentinel'd** – *guarded*
>
> **sooth** – *truth*
>
> **chidings** – *cries*
>
> **Snowdon** – *mountain in North Wales*
>
> **scant** – *few*
>
> **booty** – *treasure (here the kill from the hunt)*
>
> **aghast** – *horrified*
>
> **besprent** – *covered*
>
> **suppliant** – *begging*
>
> **impart** – *give*
>
> **scathe** – *injury*
>
> **rue** – *regret*
>
> **fancy** – *imagination*

Llewellyn And His Dog

The spearman heard the bugle sound,
And cheerily smiled the morn;
And many a brach, and many a hound,
Obeyed Llewellyn's horn.

And still he blew a louder blast,
And gave a louder cheer:
'Come, Gelert, come, why art thou last
Llewellyn's horn to hear!

'Oh, where does faithful Gelert roam?
The flower of all his race!
So true, so brave – a lamb at home,
A lion in the chase!'

'Twas only at Llewellyn's board
The faithful Gelert fed;
He watched, he served, he cheered his lord,
And sentinel'd his bed.

In sooth he was a peerless hound,
The gift of Royal John –
But now no Gelert could be found,
And all the chase rode on.

And now as over rocks and dells
The gallant chidings rise,
All Snowdon's craggy chaos yells
With many mingled cries.

That day Llewellyn little loved
The chase of hart or hare;
And scant and small the booty proved,
For Gelert was not there.

Unpleased Llewellyn homeward hied,
When, near the portal-seat,
His truant, Gelert, he espied,
Bounding his lord to greet.

But when he gained the castle-door,
Aghast the chieftain stood;
The hound all o'er was smeared with gore –
His lips, his fangs ran blood!

Llewellyn gazed with fierce surprise,
Unused such looks to meet,
His favourite checked his joyful guise,
And crouched and licked his feet.

Onward in haste Llewellyn passed –
And on went Gelert too –
And still, where'er his eyes were cast,
Fresh blood-gouts shocked his view!

O'erturned his infant's bed he found,
The bloodstained covert rent,
And all around, the walls and ground,
With recent blood besprent.

He called his child – no voice replied;
He searched – with terror wild;
Blood! blood! he found on every side,
But nowhere found the child!

'Hell-hound! my child's by thee devoured!'
The frantic father cried;
And, to the hilt, his vengeful sword
He plunged in Gelert's side!

His suppliant looks, as prone he fell,
No pity could impart;
But still his Gelert's dying yell,
Passed heavy o'er his heart.

Aroused by Gelert's dying yell,
Some slumberer wakened nigh:
What words the parent's joy can tell,
To hear his infant cry?

Concealed beneath a tumbled heap,
His hurried search had missed,
All glowing from his rosy sleep
The cherub-boy he kissed.

Nor scathe had he, nor harm, nor dread –
But the same couch beneath
Lay a gaunt wolf, all torn and dead –
Tremendous still in death!

Ah! what was then Llewellyn's pain,
For now the truth was clear;
The gallant hound the wolf had slain,
To save Llewellyn's heir.

Vain, vain was all Llewellyn's woe;
'Best of thy kind, adieu!
The frantic deed which laid thee low
This heart shall ever rue!'

And now a gallant tomb they raise,
With costly sculpture decked;
And marbles, storied with his praise,
Poor Gelert's bones protect.

Here never could the spearman pass,
Or forester, unmoved;
Here oft the tear-besprinkled grass
Llewellyn's sorrow proved.

And here he hung his horn and spear,
And there, as evening fell,
In fancy's ear he oft would hear
Poor Gelert's dying yell.

Hon. W. R. Spencer

UNDERSTANDING THE TEXT

Text A

1 Look at the second line, 'they stare in the mirror of the opposite seat'. What do you think the writer means by the word 'mirror' in this line?

2 Who does the old woman watch?

3 Who does the commuter watch?

Text B

4 How can we tell from the first verse that it is a good day for hunting?

5 Write down one fact that shows that Gelert is very loyal to Llewellyn.

6 When Llewellyn arrives home, what is the first sign that there is something wrong?

7 What convinces Llewellyn that Gelert must have killed his son?

8 Why does his child suddenly begin to cry?

INTERPRETING THE TEXT

Text A

9 What point do you think the writer is making about these people on the train?

How do the city people 'meet themselves'?

10 What impression do we get of these people? Are they:

unhappy   lonely   confused   fascinated by others   scared   shy

Choose the word which you think best describes them, or choose a word of your own if you prefer. Then write a sentence explaining your choice.

11 The poem shows us something about the hopes and fears of several passengers. What do we learn about the following:

Passenger	Hopes/fears
Business man	
Boy	

Text B

12 Gelert is presented as an exceptional hunting dog. Use a spider diagram to show his different qualities. For each quality, write down in brackets a quotation from the poem which illustrates it.

13 The poem was written a long time ago, and is based on a legend set in even earlier times. How can you tell? What clues are there that the poem comes from a distant period? Look for clues in **a)** what happens, **b)** the setting, **c)** the writer's use of language. Then write a short paragraph saying how you can tell that both the poem and the story it tells are old.

Text A

1 Look at some of the images the writer uses to help us visualize the scene:

   a *the crumpled old woman*

   What do you think the writer means by 'crumpled'?

   b *a starched commuter*

   What picture does this image create?

   c *his shallow eyes, pools of hopelessness*

   What do you think this image means?

2 The poem is written in just three sentences – one lasting two lines; one lasting 22 lines; and one lasting one line. What is the topic in each of these sentences?

   Sentence 1:

   Sentence 2:

   Sentence 3:

3 Look at the way the poem is structured. If you were dividing it into stanzas or sections, where would you separate them?

Text B

4 The poem is a ballad – it is written in 4-line stanzas and tells a story. Stories are usually chronological texts – they describe events in the order they happened. We expect to find connectives which help to move the plot on – words like *later*, *then*, *next*.

Write down three connectives the author uses to organize the plot in this poem.

5 Because the poem was written a long time ago, it sometimes uses sentence structures which are different from those we would use. Look at the examples below. If the text was written as a modern recount (e.g. a newspaper or police report) we would expect these phrases to be written differently. For each, suggest a new phrase that you think might be used today. The first example is done for you.

   a Nor scathe had he, nor harm, nor dread

   Modern version: *He was not injured, or harmed, or afraid*

   b But now no Gelert could be found

   c tear-besprinkled grass

   d Unpleased Llewellyn homeward hied

   e The hound all o'er was smeared with gore

6 The writer uses different techniques of imagery and figurative language.

   a Look at these examples of alliteration:

   i *And **h**ere **h**e **h**ung **h**is **h**orn and spear,*

   ii *'**H**ell-**h**ound! my child's by thee devoured!'*
   *The **f**rantic **f**ather cried*

   What is the effect of the use of alliteration in each case?

   b Gelert is described as:

   a lamb at home,
   A lion in the chase

   Why do you think the writer has used metaphor in this way rather than saying 'he was like a lamb at home and like a lion in the chase' (which would be a simile)?

   c Look at this description of the day of the hunt:

   And cheerily smiled the morn

   How does the writer's use of personification (presenting the morning as if it is a person) make the scene more vivid?

1 How important is it that Rosanne Flynn's piece is written as a poem? Would the text be very different if it were written in a descriptive paragraph of prose (everyday writing rather than poetry)? Write a description of the scene as if you are sitting on the train. Use the same characters, but add more detail about the train and the journey. You might start like this:

It is 7.40 and the train pulls out of the station. A few people in the carriage look at the people opposite. An old woman …

Then write a reflective paragraph describing the differences between the two texts.

2 *Llewellyn And His Dog* was written a long time ago and some readers may find parts of the language difficult to follow. How might it be updated for a modern audience?

Choose one stanza, such as this one:

In sooth he was a peerless hound,
The gift of Royal John -
But now no Gelert could be found,
And all the chase rode on.

Imagine it is part of a children's story written in prose, not poetry. Write the passage as it might appear, making it as clear for your readers (aged 8–11) as possible.

Write a brief paragraph describing the changes you have made. Comment on:

◆ changes to words

◆ changes to word order

◆ other changes to sentence structure

◆ anything else you altered.

Describe how your new version seems different from the original.

Extended Writing

Take a story you know well. It may be a local legend or a fairy tale, or something that has happened to a member of your family. Retell the story in a ballad form, using *Llewellyn And His Dog* as a model. Aim to:

♦ use stanzas made up of four lines each

♦ use the rhyme scheme ABAB, so that the first line rhymes with the third, and the second line rhymes with the fourth

♦ create a strong sense of rhythm

♦ use alliteration to make the descriptions vivid

♦ use imagery (such as similes, metaphor and personification) to bring the story to life.

For example, if you wanted to write on a sporting theme, you could imagine you were telling the story of the English football team who, after a long period without any success, get a new manager from overseas who leads them to World Cup victory. You might begin like this:

The team thought they could never win
The stars were all depressed
The managers shared the single sin
Of not tapping the players' best.

The fans were getting cross and sad ...

Speaking and listening
Special assignment

Investigation

A local journalist has been told that strange events have been
taking place at Lord Llewellyn's manor. She or he wants to
interview people who may know something about it. Working in
role, help the journalist to find out what has been going on.

The journalist should interview Llewellyn about the day's events,
and also the eyewitnesses (e.g. servants, other hunters) who might
know what happened.

1   Decide who should play each role: Llewellyn, his servants, the
    hunters, and the journalist.

2   Prepare for your role by thinking about what you have read in
    the ballad *Llewellyn And His Dog*, and what questions might be
    asked about the events it retells.

3   Role play your interviews, with the journalist trying to find out
    exactly what happened, and how each person feels about it.

Influential and significant texts

'Literary heritage' means the tradition of literature that has developed through history. Since the early years after the invention of printing, some texts have stood out as more important than others.

Here are a few examples of texts which have been especially important. Of course, a table like this cannot tell the whole story. It is a very small sample of texts; it mostly includes men; it focuses only on writing published in Britain. Many other writers have had an influence on literary heritage, as you will find if you continue to study English literature.

Literary heritage: a few examples

Text/writer	Period of time	Reason for the influence on others
Authorized Version of the Bible (prose)	First published 1611	Changed the nature of the English language. The language of the Bible had a huge impact on many later writers. The style was clear, beautiful and often poetic.
Shakespeare (drama)	1564–1616	Changed the English language and created memorable characters and scenes. He took stories from many sources and retold them with huge power. His language was highly creative and inventive.
Daniel Defoe (fiction)	1660–1731	Helped to invent the novel in English. He created some memorable characters (e.g. Robinson Crusoe). His biggest influence was to launch the novel, which became one of the most important forms of imaginative writing. He influenced writers like Dickens.
William Wordsworth (poetry)	1770-1850	Changed the language and subject-matter of poetry. Until Wordsworth, poetry had often been very formal, written in tight structures. Wordsworth adopted more informal language. He also wrote more directly about personal emotions.

Jane Austen (fiction)	1775–1817	Changed the English novel. Jane Austen showed how the novel could explore the private thoughts and feelings of characters, how it could reflect its society, and how writers could create main characters who were not always likeable.
Charles Dickens (fiction)	1812–1870	Brought the novel to a much wider audience. Dickens' novels were as popular as our soap operas today. He wrote them with large casts of characters, lots of scenes, a fast-paced storyline, and plenty of cliff-hangers to keep people reading.
T. S. Eliot (poetry)	1888–1965	Changed the language of poetry. Eliot wrote poetry that was often confusing, disjointed, and disturbing. He led the way for poets using highly creative language to explore feelings.
Samuel Beckett (drama)	1906–1989	Changed the language and content of drama. Beckett's plays are difficult and disturbing. Often nothing seems to happen: people just talk. Even then it is not always clear what they mean. His plays often show that life can seem puzzling, unhappy, even meaningless. His work can also be very funny.

This unit focuses on one writer's work from the literary heritage: Robert Louis Stevenson. A Scottish novelist, he is probably most famous for his tale *Dr Jekyll and Mr Hyde* (published in 1886). This is a disturbing tale of a respectable doctor (Dr Jekyll) who has an evil side (Mr Hyde) who causes terror throughout London. In this extract, an eyewitness has seen Mr Hyde trample on a child.

Dr Jekyll and Mr Hyde

OBJECTIVES

You will be studying these objectives:

- Sentence level: *starting paragraphs*, and *sentences in older texts*

- Reading: *distinguish writer's views, character, setting and mood, language choices* (how they enhance meanings), *author attitudes* (distinguishing between the author's attitudes and those of the characters), and *literary heritage*

- Writing: *develop logic* (explain a process with cause and effect), and *reflective writing* (about a text)

GLOSSARY

sordid – *unpleasant*

distained – *discoloured, spoilt*

ravages – *damage*

Juggernaut – *an image of a god dragged in procession on an enormous cart, in front of which devotees would throw themselves and be crushed*

Sawbones – *nickname for a doctor*

apothecary – *doctor (originally someone who sold medicines)*

harpy – *monster with a woman's face and body, and a bird's wings and claws*

Dr Jekyll and Mr Hyde

Two doors from one corner, on the left hand going east, the line was   1
broken by the entry of a court; and just at that point, a certain   2
sinister block of building thrust forward its gable on the street. It was   3
two storeys high; showed no window, nothing but a door on the   4
lower storey and a blind forehead of discoloured wall on the upper;   5
and bore in every feature the marks of prolonged and sordid   6
negligence. The door, which was equipped with neither bell nor   7
knocker, was blistered and distained. Tramps slouched into the   8
recess and struck matches on the panels; children kept shop upon the   9
steps; the schoolboy had tried his knife on the mouldings; and for   10
close on a generation no one had appeared to drive away these   11
random visitors or to repair their ravages.   12

Mr Enfield and the lawyer were on the other side of the by-street;   13
but when they came abreast of the entry, the former lifted up his   14
cane and pointed.   15

'Did you ever remark that door?' he asked; and when his companion   16
had replied in the affirmative, 'It is connected in my mind,' added   17
he, 'with a very odd story.'   18

'Indeed?' said Mr Utterson, with a slight change of voice, 'and what   19
was that?'   20

'Well, it was this way,' returned Mr Enfield: 'I was coming home   21
from some place at the end of the world, about three o'clock of a   22
black winter morning, and my way lay through a part of town where   23
there was literally nothing to be seen but lamps. Street after street   24
and all the folks asleep – street after street, all lighted up as if for a   25

procession, and all as empty as a church – till at last I got into that 26
state of mind when a man listens and listens and begins to long for 27
the sight of a policeman. All at once, I saw two figures: one a little 28
man who was stumping along eastward at a good walk, and the other 29
a girl of maybe eight or ten who was running as hard as she was able 30
down a cross-street. Well, sir, the two ran into one another naturally 31
enough at the corner; and then came the horrible part of the thing; 32
for the man trampled calmly over the child's body and left her 33
screaming on the ground. It sounds nothing to hear, but it was hellish 34
to see. It wasn't like a man; it was like some damned Juggernaut. I 35
gave a few halloa, took to my heels, collared my gentleman, and 36
brought him back to where there was already quite a group about the 37
screaming child. He was perfectly cool and made no resistance, but 38
gave me one look, so ugly that it brought out the sweat on me like 39
running. The people who had turned out were the girl's own family; 40
and pretty soon the doctor, for whom she had been sent, put in his 41
appearance. Well, the child was not much the worse, more 42
frightened, according to the Sawbones; and there you might have 43
supposed would be an end to it. But there was one curious 44
circumstance. I had taken a loathing to my gentleman at first sight. 45
So had the child's family, which was only natural. But the doctor's 46
case was what struck me. He was the usual cut-and-dry apothecary, 47
of no particular age and colour, with a strong Edinburgh accent, and 48
about as emotional as a bagpipe. Well, sir, he was like the rest of us: 49
every time he looked at my prisoner, I saw that Sawbones turn sick 50
and white with the desire to kill him. I knew what was in his mind, 51
just as he knew what was in mine; and killing being out of the 52
question, we did the next best. We told the man we could and would 53
make such a scandal out of this, as should make his name stink from 54
one end of London to the other. If he had any friends or any credit, 55
we undertook that he should lose them. And all the time, as we were 56
pitching it in red hot, we were keeping the women off him as best 57
we could, for they were as wild as harpies. I never saw a circle of 58
such hateful faces; and there was the man in the middle, with a kind 59
of black sneering coolness – frightened too, I could see that – but 60
carrying it off, sir, really like Satan. "If you choose to make capital 61
out of this accident," said he, "I am naturally helpless. No gentleman 62
but wishes to avoid a scene," says he. "Name your figure."' 63

Robert Louis Stevenson

UNDERSTANDING THE TEXT

1 Write down two details which show that the door at the start of the extract has not been looked after.

2 Why did Mr Enfield begin to 'long for the sight of a policeman'?

3 What did Mr Enfield do after he saw the girl get trampled?

4 What was surprising about the doctor's reaction to the man who trampled the girl?

5 The man who trampled the girl wishes to 'avoid a scene'. What does he do?

INTERPRETING THE TEXT

6 What do we learn about the character of the man who tramples the girl? Write down any details of:

  ◆ what he looks like

  ◆ how he behaves

  ◆ any particular words or phrases used to describe him.

7 How does Robert Louis Stevenson build tension in this extract? What makes us want to read on?

LANGUAGE AND STRUCTURE

1 Robert Louis Stevenson uses a number of images to help the reader to visualize people and places in his story. Look at the list of images on the next page. For each one, try to say what the description is showing us.

Example	What the image tells us about the place or character
(The streets were) as empty as a church	
It wasn't like a man; it was like some damned Juggernaut	
(The women) were as wild as harpies	
(The man who tramples the girl is) really like Satan	

2 The text was written more than 100 years ago. Find three examples of words which suggest the age of the story. Then try to think of a word we might use instead today.

3 What makes the language of this text seem old, rather than written recently?

Choose one sentence which has a different feel from the way we might write it today. Using two columns, write your chosen sentence in column 1 and then in column 2 write the sentence as we might write it today.

Underneath, write a few lines to explain your changes. Say something about:

- how you have altered the structure of the sentence

- any words you have added or deleted

- any changes you have made to the punctuation of the sentence.

4 Novels written in the past often use longer paragraphs than we do today. If you were editing this text for a modern audience, where would you divide it into new paragraphs?

a How many paragraphs would you have overall?

b Using the line numbers at the side, say where you would start each new paragraph (e.g. line 8 after 'distained') and why you would start a new paragraph (e.g. There is a new topic – the people around the door rather than the door itself).

5 One of the influential features of Robert Louis Stevenson's style is the way he uses different layers of storytelling. He tells the story of the man trampling the child through the eyes of a witness – Mr Enfield. This means that we get Mr Enfield's opinion, rather than simply a description of what happened.

Look at these two examples:

a *He was perfectly cool and made no resistance, but gave me one look, so ugly that it brought out the sweat on me like running...*

b *I never saw a circle of such hateful faces; and there was the man in the middle, with a kind of black sneering coolness - frightened too, I could see that - but carrying it off, sir, really like Satan.*

For each example, say what we learn about the man, and what we learn about Enfield's attitude to him.

The man who tramples the girl	The character of Enfield
a	
b	

WRITING ACTIVITY

By the end of this extract we are clearly supposed to dislike the man who tramples the child. How does the writer make us dislike him?

Write a paragraph explaining how the writer shapes our response. You should aim to mention:

* what the man does
* the way he is described
* the setting
* use of emotive words to create a sense of fear or repulsion
* the way the scene is presented through Mr Enfield's eyes.

Try to write your paragraph in a way that will be useful and interesting for other readers of Robert Louis Stevenson's text. Aim to build up your argument logically, giving quotations to show how the writer achieves his effects.

EXTENDED WRITING

Do some research into English literary heritage. Choose five of the names below (all of whom are listed in the national curriculum for English) and produce a poster or display which shows:

◆ something about who they were (give pictures, dates, where they lived)

◆ something about the texts they wrote (give a list of key titles, subjects, illustrations of book covers)

◆ an extract from one text (e.g. an opening paragraph)

◆ a quotation from someone about why the writer was so influential (e.g. a critic, an editor, a teacher).

Put all the different posters together to create a class display which shows some important figures in the literary heritage. You could sequence the display in order, perhaps with a time-line running across the room, to show which writers wrote in which periods.

Choose from the following authors:

Jane Austen	E. M. Forster
Charlotte Brontë	Thomas Hardy
Emily Brontë	John Keats
Robert Browning	D. H. Lawrence
Geoffrey Chaucer	Wilfred Owen
Samuel Taylor Coleridge	Mary Shelley
Daniel Defoe	William Shakespeare
Charles Dickens	George Bernard Shaw
John Donne	Robert Louis Stevenson
George Eliot	William Wordsworth
T. S. Eliot	

Addressing the reader directly

Introduction

When writers tell stories, they can choose to use any of a huge range of styles. These include either telling or showing. When a writer **tells** the reader something it might sound like this:

Many years ago there was an old, neglected castle ...

This approach will use description. Or the writer might address the reader directly, like this:

I want to tell you about an old, neglected castle ...

Showing usually involves getting readers to work out more details for themselves, like this:

The weeds around the castle had grown longer ...

This doesn't say directly that the castle is old or neglected, but hints at it by referring to weeds.

This unit looks at the way writers tell stories and, in particular, how they might address the reader directly to get us involved in the storyline.

The Umbrella Man

> ### OBJECTIVES
> You will be studying the following objectives:
> * Sentence level: *variety of sentence structure*
> * Reading: *development of key ideas*
> * Writing: *narrative commentary*

The Umbrella Man

I'm going to tell you about a funny thing that happened to my mother and me yesterday evening. I am twelve years old and I'm a girl. My mother is thirty-four but I am nearly as tall as her already.

Yesterday afternoon, my mother took me up to London to see the dentist. He found one hole. It was in a back tooth and he filled it without hurting me too much. After that, we went to a café. I had a banana split and my mother had a cup of coffee. By the time we got up to leave, it was about six o'clock.

When we came out of the café it had started to rain. 'We must get a taxi,' my mother said. We were wearing ordinary hats and coats, and it was raining quite hard.

'Why don't we go back into the café and wait for it to stop?' I said. I wanted another of those banana splits. They were gorgeous.

'It isn't going to stop,' my mother said. 'We must get home.'

We stood on the pavement in the rain, looking for a taxi. Lots of them came by but they all had passengers inside them. 'I wish we had a car with a chauffeur,' my mother said.

Just then a man came up to us. He was a small man and he was pretty old, probably seventy or more. He raised his hat politely and said to my mother, 'Excuse me, I do hope you will excuse me . . .' He had a fine white moustache and bushy white eyebrows and a wrinkly pink face. He was sheltering under an umbrella which he held high over his head.

'Yes?' my mother said, very cool and distant.

'I wonder if I could ask a small favour of you,' he said. 'It is only a very small favour.'

I saw my mother looking at him suspiciously. She is a suspicious person, my mother. She is especially suspicious of two things – strange men and boiled eggs. When she cuts the top off a boiled egg, she pokes around inside it with her spoon as though expecting to find a mouse or something. With strange men, she has a golden rule which says, 'The nicer the man seems to be, the more suspicious you must become.' This little old man was particularly nice. He was polite. He was wellspoken. He was well-dressed. He was a real gentleman. The reason I knew he was a gentleman was because of his shoes. 'You can always spot a gentleman by the shoes he wears,' was another of my mother's favourite sayings. This man had beautiful brown shoes.

'The truth of the matter is,' the little man was saying, 'I've got myself into a bit of a scrape. I need some help. Not much I assure you. It's almost nothing, in fact, but I do need it. You see, madam, old people like me often become terribly forgetful . . .'

My mother's chin was up and she was staring down at him along the full length of her nose. It was a fearsome thing, this frosty-nosed stare of my mother's. Most people go to pieces completely when she gives it to them. I once saw my own headmistress begin to stammer and simper like an idiot when my mother gave her a really foul frosty-noser. But the little man on the pavement with the umbrella over his head didn't bat an eyelid. He gave a gentle smile and said, 'I beg you to believe me, madam, that I am not in the habit of stopping ladies in the street and telling them my troubles.'

'I should hope not,' my mother said.

I felt quite embarrassed by my mother's sharpness. I wanted to say to her, 'Oh, mummy, for heaven's sake, he's a very very old man, and he's sweet and polite, and he's in some sort of trouble, so don't be so beastly to him.' But I didn't say anything.

The little man shifted his umbrella from one hand to the other. 'I've never forgotten it before,' he said.

'You've never forgotten what?' my mother asked sternly.

'My wallet,' he said. 'I must have left it in my other jacket. Isn't that the silliest thing to do?'

'Are you asking me to give you money?' my mother said.

'Oh, good gracious me, no!' he cried. 'Heaven forbid I should ever do that!'

'Then what *are* you asking?' my mother said. 'Do hurry up. We're getting soaked to the skin here.'

'I know you are,' he said. 'And that is why I'm offering you this umbrella of mine to protect you, and to keep forever, if … if only …'

'If only what?' my mother said.

'If only you would give me in return a pound for my taxi-fare just to get me home.'

My mother was still suspicious. 'If you had no money in the first place,' she said, 'then how did you get here?'

'I walked,' he answered. 'Every day I go for a lovely long walk and then I summon a taxi to take me home. I do it every day of the year.'

'Why don't you walk home now?' my mother asked.

'Oh, I wish I could,' he said. 'I do wish I could. But I don't think I could manage it on these silly old legs of mine. I've gone too far already.'

My mother stood there chewing her lower lip. She was beginning to melt a bit, I could see that. And the idea of getting an umbrella to shelter under must have tempted her a good deal.

'It's a lovely umbrella,' the little man said.

'So I've noticed,' my mother said.

'It's silk,' he said.

'I can see that.'

'Then why don't you take it, madam,' he said. 'It cost me over twenty pounds, I promise you. But that's of no importance so long as I can get home and rest these old legs of mine.'

I saw my mother's hand feeling for the clasp of her purse. She saw me watching her. I was giving her one of my *own* frosty-nosed looks this time and she knew exactly what I was telling her. Now listen, mummy, I was telling her, you simply *musn't* take advantage of a tired old man in this way. It's a rotten thing to do. My mother paused and looked back at me. Then she said to the little man, 'I don't think it's quite right that I should take an umbrella from you worth twenty pounds. I think I'd better just *give* you the taxi-fare and be done with it.'

'No, no, no!' he cried. 'It's out of the question! I wouldn't dream of it! Not in a million years! I would never accept money from you like that! Take the umbrella, dear lady, and keep the rain off your shoulders!'

My mother gave me a triumphant sideways look. There you are, she was telling me. You're wrong. He *wants* me to have it.

She fished into her purse and took out a pound note. She held it out to the little man. He took it and handed her the umbrella. He pocketed the pound, raised his hat, gave a quick bow from the waist, and said, 'Thank you, madam, thank you.' Then he was gone.

'Come under here and keep dry, darling', my mother said. 'Aren't we lucky. I've never had a silk umbrella before, I couldn't afford it.'

'Why were you so horrid to him in the beginning?' I asked.

'I wanted to satisfy myself he wasn't a trickster,' she said. 'And I did. He was a gentleman. I'm very pleased I was able to help him.'

'Yes, mummy,' I said.

Roald Dahl

UNDERSTANDING THE TEXT

1 Look again at the first paragraph. Write down three facts we learn about the narrator of the story.

2 From the story as a whole, write down three things the narrator likes about the old man.

3 Why is the mother suspicious about the old man?

4 Why does she hesitate about whether to pay the old man for the umbrella?

INTERPRETING THE TEXT

5 Look at paragraph 9. The old man says: 'I wonder if I could ask a small favour of you …'. The writer then adds several paragraphs describing the mother's reaction before showing us what the favour is. What effect does he create by doing this?

6 Do you think the writer wants us to admire the mother, or to dislike her? How does he present her?

LANGUAGE AND STRUCTURE

1 Look more closely at the way the writer presents this story. He could have started it at the beginning of paragraph 2: 'Yesterday afternoon …'. Instead he begins with a direct address to the reader.

Why do you think he does this?

2 In the first paragraph the writer directly tells us information about the characters: 'I am twelve years old and I'm a girl …' Decide which of the reasons below you most agree with, and explain why:

a This approach makes the story more interesting.

b This approach makes the story seem more believable.

c This approach makes the relationship between the mother and daughter seem more realistic.

d This approach makes the story feel as if it's drawn from real life rather than made up.

Start your response:

The statement I most agree with is … because …

3 Sometimes fiction writers use description: 'I saw my mother looking at him suspiciously'. Sometimes they use commentary: 'She is a suspicious person, my mother'.

Find other examples of description and commentary in this text.

4 Some writers try to avoid commentary. They prefer to 'show' rather than 'tell'. For example, rather than telling the reader that a character is very mean, the writer may just show them not prepared to lend money to a close friend.

How could Roald Dahl have *shown* the mother being suspicious rather than telling us 'she is a suspicious person'?

5 The writer presents two different views of the old man from the start of the story. How can you tell that he expects us to agree with the narrator's view rather than the mother's?

6 The writer uses a variety of sentence structures, including very short ones such as: 'They were gorgeous'. Find another example of a short, simple sentence in this text and describe its effect on the reader.

WRITING ACTIVITY

Rewrite the opening of the story so that you *show* the reader what the narrator is like without directly telling us that she is a girl aged 12, or that her mother is aged 34.

Then write a sentence or two explaining how easy or difficult it was to write your new opening paragraph, and how well you think it worked.

Unit 6

EXTENDED WRITING

Take the story situation below. Write two versions of the story's opening sequence, using the two sets of style hints.

Story situation

X and Y (you can think up the names) have been friends since they were very young. Recently X has noticed that Y seems to be behaving differently. X wonders whether Y is unhappy, whether there are problems at home, whether she or he is under some other kind of pressure. X wants to discuss the situation but can't quite pluck up the courage. Then one night after school X sees Y talking to two older men. They look suspicious. Y looks as if she or he is arguing with them. X sees Y walking away a few minutes later and it seems as if Y has been crying.

Story styles

Story style 1	Story style 2
Tell the story in third-person style (using *she* or *he*)	Tell the story in the first person ('I')
Use the past tense	Tell it as though you are X
Show things rather than telling us – e.g. avoid saying 'Y was behaving strangely …'	Address the reader directly: 'I am worried about …'
	You might use a diary style
Decide at which point to start the story – e.g. in class earlier that day, in childhood when the two friends are playing, or with Y meeting the two men	You might try using the present tense
	Use commentary as well as description: 'Y was behaving really strangely today …'

Talk to a partner about the two story openings you have written. Which does he or she prefer and why?

Now write a one-paragraph commentary describing how well you think the two story openings work, and what you have learnt.

In your commentary, focus on:

◆ the way you present the characters

◆ how much description you use

◆ the technique of commenting directly to the reader.

Figurative language

Writers often use language in imaginative, unexpected ways to present scenes and characters. This is called **figurative language**. You find it in all kinds of writing, including fiction, poetry and drama, as well as non-fiction text types like advertising. This unit explores figurative language in fiction and poetry.

Figurative language might include the following:

Alliteration

This is the term used to describe a series of words next to or near each other, which all begin with the same consonant sound. This creates particular effects, e.g. **W**et, **w**indy **w**eather.

Emotive language

This is language that provokes a strong emotional response. Emotive words connected with fear might include: *dread, horror, terror*. Less emotive words might be *afraid, worried, scared*.

Hyperbole

This is exaggeration for the sake of emphasis or comic effect, e.g. *the journey took **forever***.

Metaphor

Metaphor is the most common figure of speech. In metaphor, one thing is compared to another without using the linking words 'like' or 'as', so it is more direct than simile – one thing is actually said to be the other. For example, *My brother's room **is a pig sty***.

Onomatopoeia

This is a term which refers to words that are thought to sound like the things they describe, e.g. *buzz, creak, murmur, bang, crash*.

Oxymoron

This is a figure of speech that combines two contrasting terms, e.g. *bitter sweet, living death, delicious hatred*.

Pathetic fallacy

This means using natural settings to help describe the feelings of characters – e.g. a bright summer's day when someone is happy, a storm when terrified, rain when sad.

Personification

This is a form of figurative language in which animals, inanimate objects and abstract ideas are addressed or described as if they were human, e.g. *The sun refused to show its face.*

Simile

In a simile, two things are compared using the linking words 'like' or 'as'. For example, *My brother's room is **as** messy **as** a pig-sty.*

Introduction

E. Annie Proulx writes novels set in some bleak landscapes in North America. The following extract is taken from her novel *The Shipping News*. It is set in the remotest corner of Newfoundland, up against the Arctic Circle. In this scene, the hero Quoyle tries to rescue someone apparently drowned at sea.

The Shipping News

OBJECTIVES

These are the objectives you will be studying:

- Word level: *use linguistic terms* (terms that are used to analyse language) and *figurative vocabulary*
- Sentence level: *variety of sentence structure*
- Reading: *development of key ideas*
- Writing: *figurative language*

GLOSSARY

grapnel – *hooked grappling tool*

RCMP – *the Canadian national police force*

yawed – *turned from side to side*

broached – *took in water*

The Shipping News

There was no way down to the body unless he leaped into the foam. If he had brought a rope and grapnel … He began to climb back up the cliff. It struck him the man might have fallen from where he now climbed. Yet more likely from a boat. Tell someone.

Up on the headland again he ran. His sides aching. Tell someone about the dead man. When he reached the house it would take still another hour to drive around the bay to the RCMP station. Faster in the boat. The wind at his back swept his hair forward so that the ends snapped at his eyes. At first he felt the cold on his neck, but as he trotted over the rock he flushed with heat and had to unzip his jacket. A long time to get to the dock.

Caught in the urgency of it, that yellow corpse shuttling in and out, he cast free and set straight across the bay for Killick-Claw. As though there were still a chance to save the man. In ten minutes, as he moved out of the shelter of the lee shore and into the wind, he knew he'd made a mistake.

Had never had his boat in such rough water. The swells came at him broadside from the mouth of the bay, crests like cruel smiles. The boat rolled, rose up, dropped with sickening speed into the troughs. Instinctively he changed course, taking the waves at an angle on his bow. But now he was headed for a point northeast of Killick-Claw. Somewhere he would have to turn and make an east-southeast run for the harbour. In his experience Quoyle did not understand how to tack a zigzag across the bay, a long run with the wind and waves on his bow and then a short leg with the wind on his quarter. Halfway across he made a sudden turn toward Killick-Claw, presented his low, wide stern to the swell.

The boat wallowed about and a short length of line slid out from under the seat. It was knotted at one end, kinked and crimped at the other as if old knots had finally been untied. For the first time Quoyle got it – there was meaning in the knotted strings.

The boat pitched and plunged headlong, the bow digging into the loud water while the propeller raced. Quoyle was frightened. Each time, he lost the rudder and the boat yawed. In a few minutes his voyage ended. The bow struck like an axe, throwing the stern high. At once a wave seized, threw the boat broadside to the oncoming sea. It broached. Capsized. And Quoyle was flying under water.

In fifteen terrifying seconds he learned to swim well enough to reach the capsized boat and grasp the stilled propeller shaft. His weight pulled one side of the upturned stern down and lifted the bow a little, enough to catch an oncoming wave that twisted the boat, turned it over and filled it. Quoyle, tumbling through the transparent sea again, saw the pale boat below him, sinking, drifting casually down, the familiar details of its construction and paint becoming indistinct as it passed into the depths.

He came to the surface gasping, half blinded by some hot stuff in his eyes, and saw bloody water drip.

'Stupid,' he thought, 'stupid to drown with the children so small.' No life jackets, no floating oars, no sense. Up he rose on a swell, buoyed by body fat and a lungful of air. He was floating. A mile and a half from either shore Quoyle was floating in the cold waves. The piece of knotted twine drifted in front of him and about twenty feet away a red box bobbed – the plastic cooler for the ice he'd forgotten. He thrashed to the cooler through a flotilla of wooden matches that must have fallen into

the boat from the grocery bag. He remembered buying them. Guessed they would wash up on shore someday, tiny sticks with the heads washed away. Where would he be?

He gripped the handles of the cooler, rested his upper breast on the cover. Blood from his forehead or hairline but he didn't dare let go of the box to reach up and touch the wound. He could not remember being struck. The boat must have caught him as it went over.

The waves seemed montainous but he rose and fell with them like a chip, watched for the green curlers that shoved him under, the lifting sly crests that drove seawater into his nose.

The tide had been almost out when he saw the dead man, perhaps two hours ago. It must be on the turn now. His watch was gone.

E. Annie Proulx

UNDERSTANDING THE TEXT

1 Quoyle sees the person in the water but does not immediately try to rescue him. Why not?

2 Early on, Quoyle realizes he has made a mistake. What is it?

3 What are we told about Quoyle's ability to sail the boat?

4 In the water, what does Quoyle hold onto to stay afloat?

INTERPRETING THE TEXT

5 How does the writer show that Quoyle is anxious in the first two paragraphs?

6 The writer describes Quoyle, and shows us his thoughts (' "Stupid," he thought …'). What impression do you get of Quoyle from the extract?

LANGUAGE AND STRUCTURE

1 Look at these descriptions used by the writer, both of which contain similes:

The swells came at him broadside from the mouth of the bay, crests like cruel smiles.

The waves seemed mountainous but he rose and fell with them like a chip, watched for the green curlers that shoved him under, the lifting sly crests that drove seawater into his nose.

    a Write down the phrases that contain similes.

    b Notice how the writer describes the sea and waves. What technique does she use to make them seem threatening?

2 The writer sometimes uses very short sentences, and sometimes minor sentences (ones that do not contain a verb).

It struck him the man might have fallen from where he now climbed. **Yet more likely from a boat. Tell someone.**

Up on the headland again he ran. **His sides aching.**

[The boat] broached. Capsized. And Quoyle was flying under water.

    a Rewrite these three examples using a more conventional (usual) style of punctuation.

    b Say why you think the writer uses this style of very short sentences, and minor sentences. What effect does it have?

3 The writer structures the story to show how events lead to Quoyle being pitched into the rough sea. Look at paragraphs 1–6, and say what the topic is for each paragraph.

WRITING ACTIVITY

The writer describes events in a dramatic way. How would Quoyle himself later look back on what happened? Imagine that he is saved from the sea and recovers. Write the diary entry he might have written, describing how he came to be in the sea in the first place, and the thoughts and feelings he had. You could also make up how he might have been rescued, and describe that.

EXTENDED WRITING

In the nineteenth century, engineers built a series of lighthouses around the coast of the British Isles. These were often built in places exposed to stormy seas, and involved dangerous journeys to isolated outcrops of rock.

Write a story or poem which uses figurative language to show these humans battling against nature.

Imagine a small team of people busy working on a small area of rock. The sky begins to darken and a terrible storm is clearly brewing. They can either try to escape by sailing their ship back to the mainland, or stay put and wait out the storm, sheltering in a tiny hut.

Use figurative language to capture the power of the storm and the desperate fear of the workers.

Write either in prose (as the opening of a story) or in verse (a poem).

The focus should be on the power of your language, rather than on the storyline itself. Try to give your language the power to show how terrible the storm really is. Use some of the language features mentioned in this unit: alliteration, emotive language, hyperbole, metaphor, onomatopoeia, oxymoron, personification, and simile.

Establishing tone

Introduction

Writers can sometimes create powerful effects in their work by using language to hint at meanings rather than stating them directly. Think, for example, how sarcasm works in everyday conversation. You and a friend might be talking about someone else. One of you might say: 'That's a really fashionable haircut he's got'. Written on paper, the reader would assume that you meant what you said. But in speech, the tone of your voice might show that you mean the exact opposite – that it's not fashionable at all.

In speech we show sarcasm through intonation, the way we move our voices up and down. In writing it's more complex.

This unit looks at the way a writer can create irony (the meaning beneath the surface being different from the meaning on the surface). It looks at the concept of tone – the way a writer's voice can help us to know her or his attitude to what is described.

Henry Reed's poem was written about the experience of being a soldier. It evokes the regular, repetitive drills and practices soldiers have to do – here, taking a rifle apart. Think about the tone of voice that should be used for reading the poem aloud.

Naming of Parts

OBJECTIVES

You will be studying the following objectives:

- Word level: *ironic use of words*

- Reading: *bias and objectivity, implied and explicit meanings*, and *development of key ideas*

- Writing: *figurative language*, and *establish the tone*

- Speaking and listening: *hidden messages, work in role*, and *collaborative presentation*

Before reading

Work in pairs to read the poem aloud. Look at each stanza in two
parts. One of you read the first four lines of each stanza as if you
are a sergeant major on a parade ground. Then, from the fourth
line where the new sentence begins, your partner should read the
rest in a gentler way. This will help you to explore the contrasting
tones used in the poem.

> GLOSSARY
>
> **Japonica** – *a plant with pink/red flowers*

Naming of Parts

Today we have naming of parts. Yesterday,
We had daily cleaning. And tomorrow morning,
We shall have what to do after firing. But today,
Today we have naming of parts. Japonica
Glistens like coral in all of the neighbouring gardens,
And today we have naming of parts.

This is the lower sling swivel. And this
Is the upper sling swivel, whose use you will see,
When you are given your slings. And this is the piling swivel,
Which in your case you have not got. The branches
Hold in the gardens their silent, eloquent gestures,
Which in our case we have not got.

This is the safety-catch, which is always released
With an easy flick of the thumb. And please do not let me
See anyone using his finger. You can do it quite easy
If you have any strength in your thumb. The blossoms
Are fragile and motionless, never letting anyone see
Any of them using their finger.

And this you can see is the bolt. The purpose of this
Is to open the breech, as you see. We can slide it
Rapidly backwards and forwards: we call this
Easing the spring. And rapidly backwards and forwards
The early bees are assaulting and fumbling the flowers:
They call it easing the Spring.

They call it easing the Spring: it is perfectly easy
If you have any strength in your thumb: like the bolt,
And the breech, and the cocking-piece, and the point of balance,
Which in our case we have not got; and the almond-blossom
Silent in all of the gardens and the bees going backwards and forwards,
For today we have naming of parts.

Henry Reed

UNDERSTANDING THE TEXT

1 Who do you think is the narrator of the first part of each stanza?

2 Who do you think the narrator is addressing?

3 The poet uses some technical words to do with rifles. Write down two examples.

4 He also uses specific names of flowers and plants. Write down two examples.

INTERPRETING THE TEXT

5 Look again at the first stanza. The writer uses the adverbs 'today', 'yesterday' and 'tomorrow'. Why do you think he refers to the past and future in this way?

6 What can we tell about the poet's attitude to the activity of naming the parts of rifles? Is he objective about it and merely presenting the scene, or does he have a message for the reader? Finish the sentence below which you think best sums up his response:

a He thinks the activity is boring but necessary because …

b He thinks the activity is pointless because …

c He thinks the activity is very repetitive because …

d He thinks the activity seems unnatural because …

e He thinks the activity is mindless but better than being at war because …

7 What do you like or dislike about the poem?

LANGUAGE AND STRUCTURE

1 Look again at the first stanza. The writer uses the sentence 'Today we have naming of parts' three times. Why do you think he repeats it like this?

2 Each stanza has a similar structure: the first four lines describe the process of naming the parts of a rifle; the last lines describe nature.

   a What do you notice about words from the first part of each stanza that are repeated in the last part?

   b What tone of voice should be used for the first part of each verse?

   c What tone of voice should be used for the repeated words in the second part?

3 What do you notice about the vocabulary the writer uses in the different sections of each verse?

4 The poem is unusual becauses it uses 'we' and 'you', so that it sounds like a speech or discussion. How does this help the writer to show his attitude?

5 Put together a rehearsed reading of the poem. Work in pairs and practise getting the tone just right. Perform it as if it is a play.

WRITING ACTIVITY

Write a brief character description of whoever the poem is about. Who, for you, is the central character? Is it a sergeant-major, or a raw recruit?

Imagine your character and write a paragraph about him based on your response to the poem. You might use similes or metaphors to make your description vivid.

EXTENDED WRITING

Write a text called 'I love homework' (or something similar). Use it to experiment with tone of voice. You could write it as a poem, a monologue or dialogue.

On the surface, the text should seem as if it is genuinely saying 'I love homework'. The message to the reader should be, in fact, the opposite – that a lot of homework can be repetitive, boring, and exhausting.

Think about how you might create this contrast in meaning. How will you structure the writing?

You could write it in two parts: one spoken to a teacher, or by a teacher; the other, the thoughts of the pupil spoken inside her or his head.

Don't worry too much about rhythm and rhyme. The idea is to explore the tone of the text, to show an underlying meaning which differs from the surface meaning.

Here are some possible starting points:

A

I love homework
(I'd only be watching TV, or out cycling, or learning something in the real world)
I love all the writing
(I'd only be writing to my friends or keeping in touch with a long-lost auntie) …

B

I recommend homework
It's what makes me strong
Without all that practice
How would I know I was wrong? …

C

Tonight for homework you'll need to finish this poem
(I thought poems were creative things)
You'll need to write at least 15 lines
(Whatever happened to free verse?) …

Updating traditional tales

Introduction

Some writers like to create their own characters and stories from scratch. Others work with existing tales. Shakespeare, for example, drew on stories from history and legend for almost all of his plays. Many other writers have done the same. Film-makers, also, often take material from the past and explore it for a modern audience. That is why we often have more than one version of a famous story (say, about the *Titanic*) – because each new generation retells the story in its own way.

Myths and legends lend themselves to this treatment. This unit looks at a version of the legend of King Arthur, one of England's earliest rulers. The author, Kevin Crossley-Holland, is famous for his reworking of legends. He retells this story through the eyes of Arthur himself, the boy who will one day become king.

Legends have their roots in a tradition of spoken stories, where people would pass on tales by word of mouth. Sometimes, therefore, even with modern writers, the storytelling style feels like spoken English.

Arthur the King

OBJECTIVES

These are the objectives you will be studying:

- Word level: *use linguistic terms* (terms that are used to analyse language), and *figurative vocabulary*
- Sentence level: *variety of sentence structure*
- Reading: *literary conventions*
- Writing: *figurative language*, and *experiment with conventions*

Arthur the King

This falling snow is like an old man. It keeps forgetting itself, and wandering sideways. It doesn't really want to touch the ground. And now that the sun is shining, hazy, away in the west, the flakes look so frail you can almost see through them.

Sir Ector told me it was snowing when I was born. He said it was a fierce winter. Well, there have been many fierce winters since then: axe-winters, wolf-winters. There always will be.

Before my life ends, I want to describe my beginning – or, at least, the day that changed everything. I was twelve. So Kay, my elder brother, would have been six– no, seventeen. At any rate, I'm sure he had just been knighted, on All-Hallows' Day.

For several months after the death of King Uther – Uther Pendragon – the island of Britain had no king. True, Uther and Igraine, his queen, did have a son, but he had been entrusted to foster-parents when he was a baby, and only two people knew who they were: one was the old king himself, and he had gone to earth, like fallen snow; the other was the magician Merlin, and he wasn't telling.

When Uther died, everyone expected the foster-parents to claim the throne for their son, but this couple didn't realize they had the king's child in their care. So then the knights of the island began to talk and argue and lobby and squabble.

The Archbishop was worried. 'Our country needs a king,' he said, 'just as a king needs his fighting men and working men and praying men. We're like a ship without a rudder.'

Old Merlin agreed. He told the Archbishop to announce a tournament for New Year's Day, and then a great gathering at St Paul's, to choose the new king.

'Can I come?' I asked my father.

'You?' said Ector. 'I don't see why not.'

Kay wrinkled up his nose.

'Be fair, Kay!' said Ector. 'He's twelve. It's time he got the feel of things.'

On our way through London to our father's house, we saw quite a crowd of people in St Paul's churchyard. Sir Brastias was there! And Sir Tristram! And several dozen Londoners.

They had all gathered round a marvel: close to the east wall of the cathedral, there was a square plinth of shining green marble. A huge anvil had been set into the marble, and stuck into the anvil was a great gleaming sword.

Round the marble there were letters of gold. I read them for myself:

WHOEVER PULLS THIS SWORD

FROM THIS STONE AND ANVIL

IS THE TRUE-BORN KING

OF ALL BRITAIN

My father walked round the plinth. 'Where has this come from, then?' he said.

'Damned if I know!' said Brastias. He was copper-faced, and his nose was red.

'Well! What about it?' said my father.

'I can't move the damned thing,' said Brastias. 'How about you? How about it, King Ector?'

'How about King Kay?' said my brother.

Brastias looked at Kay and snorted. 'King Kay? King Kiss-curl, you mean! Never!'

First my father and then Kay stepped up on to the plinth and tried to pull the sword from the stone. But they couldn't do it. They couldn't move it a hair's breadth, and neither could any other knight who came to the churchyard.

I did wish I could try . . . But I wasn't a knight! I was only twelve.

Knights from moor and mountain, knights from marsh and fen: on New Year's morning, knights from all over the island armed themselves for the tournament.

I helped Kay put on his padded jacket and breastplate and thigh-plates and greaves and metal boots and, last of all, his helmet.

My father's servants, meanwhile, groomed and saddled our horses and tied Ector's and Kay's colours to their lances.

Just before we reached the tournament fields outside the city walls, Kay stood up in his saddle.

'My sword!' he exclaimed, clutching his sheath. 'It's gone!'

'Gone?' said Ector.

'I've left it behind,' wailed Kay. And then he rounded on me. 'You dressed me! Surely you noticed!'

'I … I …'

'It's not his fault,' said Ector.

'Go and get it!' said Kay. 'I need it. Please!'

I didn't want to turn my back on the distant shouts and braying trumpets, but I didn't want to let Kay down either. This was his first fighting tournament, and you can't fight without a sword. So I wheeled round and galloped back into London.

But when I got to my father's house, there was no one there – all the servants had gone to the tournament.

The door was locked; the windows were barred; I couldn't get in.

'What can I do?' I said. 'Kay must have a sword today.'

That was when I thought of the great gleaming blade: the sword in the stone.

I rode to the churchyard – there was nobody about; I tied my horse to the stile; I stepped up to the green marble plinth; I put my hand around the beautiful pommel, inlaid with precious stones.

Perhaps I was nervous, was I? Excited? What I remember now is such belief: a crowd of sparrows rushed across the churchyard, and I was confident and determined and joyous.

I scarcely had to pull the sword. It slid out of the anvil and flashed in the sunlight.

There was no time to waste! I galloped back to the tournament fields and gave the sword to my brother. He looked at it very carefully, then he looked at me, and his eyes brightened. I've seen that look of Kay's a hundred times. 'Father!' he called. 'Look at this!'

Ector came ambling over. 'You're back,' he said.

'Do you recognize it?' demanded Kay.

My father didn't say anything. He just stared at the sword.

'I'm the true-born king of all Britain,' crowed Kay.

'Where did you get that sword?' my father asked me.

'From the stone,' I replied. 'The house was locked and I couldn't get in, and Kay needs a sword for the tournament. It came out of the stone easily.'

'You?' said my father in a low voice. 'We're going back to the churchyard now.'

Kay and I weren't at all happy to be dragged away from the tournament, but there was nothing we could do about it. We had to turn our backs on all the excited hubbub, the brazen trumpets and the armed knights tilting and riding their challenges. We had to follow our father back into London.

Kevin Crossley-Holland

UNDERSTANDING THE TEXT

1 Look at the second paragraph. The narrator says '… it was snowing when I was born'. Who is the narrator of the story?

2 How old was the narrator on the day that his life changed?

3 What does the Archbishop mean when he says 'we're like a ship without a rudder'?

4 Why does Kay become angry with his brother?

5 How does the narrator feel when he tries pulling the sword from the stone?

INTERPRETING THE TEXT

6 Look at the opening sentence, a simile comparing the snow to an old man. What do you think the writer means by this?

7 Look more closely at the first section of the story. How does the writer make the reader want to read on?

8 Legends are usually set in a time long ago. How does this writer show that the story is set far in the past? Look for clues about:

   ♦ things that happen in the story

   ♦ the way people behave and are dressed

   ♦ the language used by the writer.

9 What impression do you get of the narrator in the story? Is he:

cocky   arrogant   innocent   foolhardy   pleasant   ambitious   nervous

Choose the word that best sums him up. Then write a sentence explaining your choice.

LANGUAGE AND STRUCTURE

1 Look again at the first sentence of the text. The writer uses the determiner 'this' rather than 'the'. What effect does this have?

2 At various points in the text the writer uses repetition of phrase structures, like this:

Well, there have been many fierce winters since then: **axe-winters, wolf-winters**.

So then the knights of the island began to **talk and argue and lobby and squabble**.

Knights from *moor and mountain,* **knights from** *marsh and fen …*

Use any of these examples and describe the effect of this repetition.

3 The writer uses some long, complex sentences like this:

When Uther died, everyone expected the foster-parents to claim the throne for their son, but this couple didn't realize they had the king's child in their care.

He also uses short, simple sentences:

Old Merlin agreed.

Find a passage where a long and complex sentence is used near a short one, and describe the effects this has.

4 In some places the story feels as if it is being spoken to us rather than written down. Find an example, and explain what makes it seem like a spoken text.

> ## HINTS
>
> Look at:
> - the way the reader is addressed
> - the types of details included
> - how they are expressed

WRITING ACTIVITY

The story is currently told using a first-person style. This means that the narrator tells us the story directly. Legends are usually told in a more impersonal style – for example, using the third person.

Take one short extract of the story and rewrite it using the third person. Make it feel more like a traditional legend.

You might begin like this:

Many years ago the snow fell thickly. It snowed like this when young Arthur was born and there had been many similarly bitter winters since then …

You can change the style as much as you wish.

Then write two or three sentences reflecting on the changes you have made, and the ways in which your version of the story feels different.

EXTENDED WRITING

Write your own modern version of a story from the past. You might choose:

- a legend or tale from your local area
- a storyline from Shakespeare (e.g. *Macbeth*, retold in a modern way, perhaps as a thriller novel)
- an old poem retold as a piece of fiction (e.g. *The Listeners*, *The Highwayman*).

Start by thinking about your audience. Who will you write your new version for? How old will the audience be? Will they already know the story, and, if so, what difference might this make?

Then start planning your writing. Think about how you will hook the reader's attention from the start. Will you address the reader directly, or use a more detached style?

- Will you use a dual narrative?
- Will you use third or first person?
- Will you update the setting of the story – e.g. moving *Macbeth* from an old Scottish castle into a more modern location? Or will it chiefly be the language that you are updating?

Once you have completed your updated version, write a brief commentary reflecting on what you have done – for example:

- What changes have you made to the characters and storyline? How have you developed the language? How have you changed the setting?
- How pleased are you with the finished version? How well do you think it meets the needs of your target audience?

To get you started, here are three possible openings of an updated *Macbeth*. Working with a partner, discuss what you like and dislike about each one.

A Third-person description/traditional setting

The wind howled across the heath as night drew on. No one would have believed that, just hours before, this had been a place of bloodshed. A thousand men had lost their lives. Now it was dark and, except for the wind, silent ...

B First-person narration/traditional setting

If I look out from the top of the castle, the very top, I can see beyond the woods and across to a vast flat heath. I don't know which I hate more, the eerily creaking trees of the woods or the dreadful emptiness of the heath. I swore I'd never go there again. Now it looks as if I've got no choice.

C Commentary/modern setting

Where would you begin a story about evil? Not in a supermarket car park, I imagine. Not somewhere so ordinary, so undramatic. But that's where this story starts because that's where Macbeth's problems started. He was on leave, having some time off, and thought he would stock up the freezer. He drove into Tesco's as normal, past the filling station, up past the recycling centre, and something caught his eye. He assumed it was kids messing around. Shapes appearing and disappearing round the back of the bottle banks. Mind your own business, Macbeth. That's what he should have said. But that was his greatest mistake ...

Experimenting with styles

10

Introduction

Poetry comes in a huge range of styles and forms. Look down this list of just a few types of poetry:

Ballad – a narrative poem

Blank verse – verse which does not rhyme, usually written in iambic pentameter (10 beats per line)

Didactic – poetry which gives the reader advice or instruction

Dirge – a song to lament the death of a famous person

Dramatic monologue – a poem in which the speaker is not the author but a character

Eclogue – a conversation poem

Elegy – a poem to commemorate someone's death

Epic – a long narrative poem dealing with important matters

Epigram – a very short, witty poem

Epitaph – verse written on a tomb

Free verse – poetry which ignores traditional rhyme and rhythm structures

Haiku – a Japanese poem in three lines of five, seven and five syllables each

Idyll – a poem describing innocent people in ideal surroundings

Lament – a poem of mourning

Lampoon – a personal attack or caricature in verse

Lyric – a short poem expressing personal feelings

Mock heroic – a poem which describes trivial events in a very grand style

Narrative verse – a poem telling a story

Occasional verse – poetry written for a special occasion

Ode – a verse originally designed to be sung

Satire – a poem which ridicules the pomposity and vanity of humans

Sonnet – a poem of 14 lines with a particular rhyme scheme.

UNIT 10

This unit gives you chance to compare the way two different poets approach the theme of love. One poem was written in the nineteenth century, the other in the twentieth century.

Both poems explore what it is like to have loved someone and then to feel alone.

Love Poetry

> ### OBJECTIVES
>
> These are the objectives you will be studying:
>
> - Word level: *use linguistic terms* (terms that are used to analyse language), *figurative vocabulary*, and *formality and word choice*
> - Sentence level: *degrees of formality*
> - Reading: *development of key ideas*, *compare treatments of same theme*, and *literary conventions*
> - Writing: *figurative language*, and *integrate evidence* (to support your analysis)

Poem A

Sonnet

What lips my lips have kissed, and where, and why,
I have forgotten, and what arms have lain
Under my head till morning; but the rain
Is full of ghosts tonight, that tap and sigh
Upon the glass and listen for reply,
And in my heart there stirs a quiet pain
For unremembered lads that not again
Will turn to me at midnight with a cry.
Thus in the winter stands the lonely tree,
Nor knows what birds have vanished one by one,
Yet knows its boughs more silent than before:
I cannot say what loves have come and gone,
I only know that summer sang in me
A little while, that in me sings no more.

Edna St Vincent Millay

Poem B

Simple Lyric

When I think of her sparkling face
And of her body that rocked this way and that,
When I think of her laughter,
Her jubilance that filled me,
It's a wonder I'm not gone mad.

She is away and I cannot do what I want.
Other faces pale when I get close.
She is away and I cannot breathe her in.

The space her leaving has created
I have attempted to fill
With bodies that numbed upon touching,
Among them I expected her opposite,
And found only forgeries.

Her wholeness I know to be a fiction of my making,
Still I cannot dismiss the longing for her;
It is a craving for sensation new flesh
Cannot wholly calm or cancel,
It is perhaps for more than her.

At night above the parks the stars are swarming.
The streets are thick with nostalgia;
I move through senseless routine and insensitive chatter
As if her going did not matter.
She is away and I cannot breathe her in.
I am ill simply through wanting her.

Brian Patten

UNDERSTANDING THE TEXT

Poem A

1 Why is the narrator feeling sad?

2 What does she mean when she says 'the rain/Is full of ghosts tonight'?

3 What might she mean by 'unremembered lads'?

Poem B

4 Write down one detail the narrator remembers about the woman.

5 The narrator says: 'Her wholeness I know to be a fiction of my making'. What do you think he means by this?

6 At the end, what impression does the narrator give of his life now?

INTERPRETING THE TEXT

Poem A

7 The writer uses nature to show how the narrator feels. What do you think the following are supposed to symbolize?

   a Winter

   b Summer.

8 What picture do you get of the narrator – old, lonely, nostalgic, bored, unhappy? Use evidence from the poem to describe what she is like.

Poem B

9 The narrator is writing about someone who clearly means a lot to him. Why do you think the writer doesn't give her name?

10 What picture do you get of the narrator of this poem? How does he seem different from the narrator of poem A?

11 What picture do you get from the two poems of the theme of love? Do they treat it differently, or do you gain a similar picture of what love feels like?

LANGUAGE AND STRUCTURE

1 Poem A has a more formal structure than poem B. How can you tell?

2 Poem A is written as a sonnet, a 14-line poem with a particular rhyme pattern. Write down the rhyme scheme for the poem, using letters. To show which lines rhyme, use the same letter. The first part is done for you:

A B B A A ...

3 Does poem B use any rhyme?

4 Poet A structures her thoughts using connectives, such as: *And ... Thus ... Nor ... Yet.*

  a How do these connectives give the poem a formal tone?

  b Poem B also uses connectives: *When ... And ... Still.* How do these make the poem seem less formal than Poem A?

5 Look at this statement:

Poem A uses formal vocabulary and lots of references to nature. Poem B is more personal and uses less formal vocabulary.

Do you agree? Write a short paragraph comparing the choice of vocabulary used in the two poems.

6 Look at the last line of poem A, which finishes: '... that in me sings no more'. How might the writer have written this same idea if she were using a more colloquial (chatty) style?

WRITING ACTIVITY

Write a brief commentary on the two poems. Compare:

- the way they present the theme of love
- their use of metaphor
- the impression given of the two writers
- the similarities and differences in their styles.

Then say which you prefer and why. Remember to quote words and lines from the poems to support your arguments.

EXTENDED WRITING

Choose a theme from the list below. Imagine there is to be a book of poetry on that theme. Write the opening parts of three poems, using a different style for each. Use the style checklist to help you.

Themes

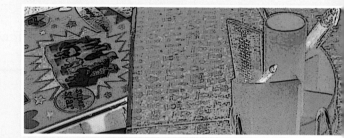

- ◆ Fear
- ◆ Falling out with a parent or friend
- ◆ Loneliness

Styles of poetry

Style checklist	Hints
Ballad – a narrative poem	Try to create a powerful rhythm. Tell the story at a rapid pace.
Didactic – a poem which gives the reader advice or instruction	Address the reader directly.
Epigram – a very short, witty poem	Aim for two or four lines.
Free verse – poetry which ignores traditional rhyme and rhythm structures	Structure your poem in any way you wish.
Haiku – a Japanese poem in three lines of five, seven and five syllables	Be strict in counting your syllables.
Lyric – a short poem expressing personal feelings	This should have a personal style, as if written about your own feelings.
Mock heroic – a poem which describes trivial events in a very grand style	Choose something insignificant like an argument over what to watch on TV, and present it as if it will lead to the world ending.

Remember that this activity is all about experimenting with poetry styles. A good starting point would be to spend some time looking though a poetry collection. This will help you to become familiar with the huge range of poetry styles that exist.

Once you have written your three fragments of poetry, you might show them as part of a class display, or talk to a small group about which style you found easiest and hardest to create.

How texts reflect their culture

11

Introduction

Sometimes when we read literature, we forget about the time and place when the text was written. For example, it can be easy to ignore the world Shakespeare lived in, which was often brutal and disturbing. Also, knowing something about the theatre of his time can help us to understand the way he wrote. For example:

◆ plays were performed in inn yards around the country, and in open-air theatres in London;

◆ performances took place by daylight;

◆ there was little scenery – instead, the words of the play had to create the scene in the audience's mind;

◆ plays would be aimed at all levels of society – so there needed to be something to appeal to everyone;

◆ the stages brought the actors very close to the audience;

◆ all the parts in a play were taken by men, never women.

The text we will study in this unit is much closer to our own times – it is by the twentieth-century children's author Enid Blyton. But it is still a reflection of its time.

Writing in the 1950s and 1960s, Enid Blyton had a huge influence on many children's early reading. After they had read her *Noddy* books, they would move on to the adventures of *The Secret Seven*, *The Famous Five*, and the *Mallory Towers* series.

With her strong emphasis on plot, Enid Blyton's adventure stories have entertained many thousands of readers. However, they also reflect the time when they were written, showing different values and attitudes – for example, in the way they present the roles of female and male characters. This extract is from one of the *Famous Five* books.

Five at Finniston Farm

OBJECTIVES

These are the objectives you will be studying:

- Word level: *formality and word choice*
- Sentence level: *change over time*
- Reading: *trace developments* (of themes and ideas), *implied and explicit meanings*, and *cultural context*
- Writing: *figurative language*, and *establish the tone*

Five at Finniston Farm

'Phew!' said Julian, mopping his wet forehead. 'What a day! Let's go and live at the Equator – it would be cool compared to this!'

He stood leaning on his bicycle, out of breath with a long steep ride up a hill. Dick grinned at him. 'You're out of training, Ju!' he said. 'Let's sit down for a bit and look at the view. We're pretty high up!'

They leaned their bicycles against a nearby gate and sat down, their backs against the lower bars. Below them spread the Dorset countryside, shimmering in the heat of the day, the distance almost lost in a blue haze. A small breeze came wandering round, and Julian sighed in relief.

'I'd never have come on this biking trip if I'd guessed it was going to be as hot as this!' he said. 'Good thing Anne didn't come – she'd have given up the first day.'

'George wouldn't have minded,' said Dick. 'She's game enough for anything.'

'Good old Georgina,' said Julian, shutting his eyes. 'I'll be glad to see the girls again. Fun to be on our own, of course – but things always seem to happen when the four of us are together.'

'*Five*, you mean,' said Dick, tipping his hat over his eyes.

'Don't forget old Timmy. What a dog! Never knew one that had such a wet lick as Tim. I say – won't it be fun to meet them all! Don't let's forget the time, Julian. Hey, wake up, ass! If we go to sleep now, we'll not be in time to meet the girls' bus.'

Julian was almost asleep. Dick looked at him and laughed. Then he looked at his watch, and did a little calculating. It was half past two.

'Let's see now – Anne and George will be on the bus that stops at Finniston Church at five past three,' he thought. 'Finniston is about a mile away, down this hill.

I'll give Julian fifteen minutes to have a nap – and hope to goodness I don't fall asleep myself!'

He felt his own eyes closing after a minute, and got up at once to walk about. The two girls and Tim *must* be met, because they would have suitcases with them, which the boys planned to wheel along on their bicycles.

The five were going to stay at a place called Finniston Farm, set on a hill above the little village of Finniston. None of them had been there before, nor even heard of it. It had all come about because George's mother had heard from an old school friend, who had told her that she was taking paying guests at her farm-house – and had asked her to recommend visitors to her. George had promptly said she would like to go there with her cousins in the summer holidays.

'Hope it's a decent place!' thought Dick, gazing down into the valley, where corn-fields waved in the little breeze. 'Anyway, we shall only be there for two weeks – and it *will* be fun to be together again.'

He looked at his watch. Time to go! He gave Julian a push. 'Hey – wake up!'

''Nother ten minutes,' muttered Julian, trying to turn over, as if he were in bed. He rolled against the gate-bars and fell on to the hard dry earth below. He sat up in surprise. 'Gosh – I thought I was in bed!' he said. 'My word, I could have gone on sleeping for hours.'

'Well, it's time to go and meet the bus,' said Dick. 'I've had to walk about all the time you were asleep, I was so afraid I'd go off myself. Come on, Julian – we really must go!'

They rode down the hill, going cautiously round the sharp corners, remembering how many times they had met herds of cows, wide farm-carts, tractors and the like, on their way through this great farming county. Ah – there was the village, at the bottom of the hill. It looked old and peaceful and half-asleep.

'Thank goodness it sells ginger-beer and ice-creams!'

said Dick, seeing a small shop with a big sign in the window. 'I feel as if I want to hang out my tongue, like Timmy does, I'm so thirsty!'

'Let's find the church and the bus-stop,' said Julian. 'I saw a spire as we rode down the hill, but it disappeared when we got near the bottom.'

'There's the bus!' said Dick, as he heard the noise of wheels rumbling along in the distance. 'Look, here it comes. We'll follow it.'

'There's Anne in it – and George, look!' shouted Julian. 'We're here exactly on time! Whoo-hoo, George!'

The bus came to a stop by the old church, and out jumped Anne and George, each with a suitcase – and out leapt old Timmy too, his tongue hanging down, very glad to be out of the hot, jerky, smelly bus.

'There are the boys!' shouted George, and waved wildly as the bus went off again. 'Julian! Dick! I'm so glad you're here to meet us!'

The two boys rode up, and jumped off their bikes, while Timmy leapt round them, barking madly. They thumped the girls on their backs, and grinned at them. 'Just the same old sixpences!' said Dick. 'You've got a spot on your chin, George, and why on *earth* have you tied your hair into a pony-tail, Anne?'

'You're not very polite, Dick,' said George, bumping him with her suitcase. 'I can't think why Anne and I looked forward so much to seeing you again. Here, take my suitcase – haven't you got any manners?'

'Plenty,' said Dick, and grabbed the case. 'I just can't get over Anne's new hair-do. I don't like it, Anne – do you Ju? Pony-tail! A donkey-tail would suit you better, Anne!'

'It's all right – it's just because the back of my neck was so hot,' said Anne, shaking her hair free in a hurry. She hated her brothers to find fault with her. Julian gave her arm a squeeze.

'Nice to see you both,' he said. 'What about some ginger-beer and ice-cream? There's a shop over there

that sells them. And I've a sudden longing for nice juicy plums!'

'You haven't said a *word* to Timmy yet,' said George, half-offended. 'He's been trotting round you and licking your hands – and he's so dreadfully hot and thirsty!'

'Shake paws, Tim,' said Dick, and Timmy politely put up his right paw. He shook hands with Julian too and then promptly went mad, careering about and almost knocking over a small boy on a bicycle.

'Come on, Tim – want an ice-cream?' said Dick, laying his hand on the big dog's head. 'Hark at him panting, George – I bet he wishes he could unzip his hairy coat and take it off! Don't you, Tim?'

'Woof!' said Tim, and slapped his tail against Dick's bare legs.

They all trooped into the ice-cream shop.

Enid Blyton

UNDERSTANDING THE TEXT

1 Where is the story set?

2 Write down the names of the members of the Famous Five.

3 Why are the children going to stay at Finniston Farm?

4 How can you tell that Dick is rude to his sister?

INTERPRETING THE TEXT

5 Write down three details from the story that show it is set in the past.

6 What do you notice about the way the characters talk which makes them sound different from the way most people speak today?

7 The text feels very sexist in places. Find an example of the way female and male characters are portrayed differently.

8 After Dick has teased Anne, 'Julian gave her arm a squeeze'. Why do you think he does this?

9 What can you tell about the different characters based on the extract? What are they like? Write down a sentence about each one.

10 What do you suppose will happen in the story? What has the writer done to prepare the reader for this?

LANGUAGE AND STRUCTURE

1 Look at the opening two paragraphs. They contain mostly dialogue. Notice how the writer uses exclamation marks at the end of many of the statements. Why do you think she uses these? What do they tell us about the way the characters speak?

2 Some of the dialogue feels old-fashioned, reflecting the time when the text was written. Look at this extract:

Don't let's forget the time, Julian. Hey, wake up, ass! If we go to sleep now, we'll not be in time to meet the girls' bus.

If you were writing the story today, how would you write this extract of dialogue?

a Write down your version.

b Write a sentence explaining what you have changed and why.

WRITING ACTIVITY

What would happen if you reversed some of the stereotypes in the story — for example, George teasing Dick about his haircut and the spot on his chin? Write a short version of the story in which:

◆ the girls are on their bikes waiting for the boys to arrive

◆ they meet them off a bus or train and tease them.

Use language in your descriptions and dialogue which shows the girls to be strong and independent, and the boys less confident. Compare different versions of the story written by people in your class.

Establishing the context

Introduction

Charles Dickens' work is admired all over the world – he is perhaps the most famous novelist in English. He wrote at an amazing rate, publishing long novels in instalments which readers would eagerly await – a little like waiting for the next episode of a modern soap opera.

As well as creating an amazing gallery of memorable characters, Dickens also used his books to show the problems of the society of his day – for example, the poverty many people suffered, the terrible prison conditions and the dreadful education system.

Here, in an extract from *Nicholas Nickleby*, he shows the terrors of a private school – Dootheboys Hall, run by Mr Wackford Squeers and his family. Here, on his first morning as a new school teacher, Nicholas sees the cruelty of the school, as Mrs Squeers fills the boys' stomachs with brimstone and treacle to spoil their appetites and stop them wanting to eat much breakfast.

Nicholas Nickleby

OBJECTIVES

You will be studying the following objectives:

- Word level: *figurative vocabulary*, and *ironic use of words*

- Sentence level: *complex sentences*, *colons and semi-colons*, *grouping sentences* (into paragraphs), and *change over time*

- Reading: *versatile reading* (searching for meaning using a range of strategies), *implied and explicit meanings*, *historical context*, and *cultural context*

- Writing: *figurative language*, and *establish the tone*

GLOSSARY

aversion – *dislike*

dogged – *constant*

malefactors – *criminals*

mercenary – *working only for money, grasping*

incipient – *early, just beginning*

brimstone – *sulphur*

corporal – *physical*

appropriation – *theft*

rueful – *sad*

physicking – *dosing with medicines*

distended – *filled out*

locomotion – *movement*

disconcerted – *concerned*

Nicholas Nickleby

'There,' said the schoolmaster as they stepped in together; 'this is our shop, Nickleby!'

It was such a crowded scene, and there were so many objects to attract attention, that, at first, Nicholas stared about him, really without seeing anything at all. By degrees, however, the place resolved itself into a bare and dirty room, with a couple of windows, whereof a tenth part might be of glass, the remainder being stopped up with old copy-books and paper. There were a couple of long old rickety desks, cut and notched, and inked, and damaged, in every possible way; two or three forms; a detached desk for Squeers; and another for his assistant. The ceiling was supported, like that of a barn, by cross-beams and rafters; and the walls were so stained and discoloured, that it was impossible to tell whether they had ever been touched with paint or whitewash.

But the pupils – the young noblemen! How the last faint traces of hope, the remotest glimmering of any good to be derived from his efforts in this den, faded from the mind of Nicholas as he looked in dismay around! Pale and haggard faces, lank and bony figures, children with the countenances of old men, deformities with irons upon their limbs, boys of stunted growth, and others whose long meagre legs would hardly bear their stooping bodies, all crowded on the view together; there were the bleared eye, the hare-lip, the crooked foot, and every ugliness or distortion that told of unnatural aversion conceived by parents for their offspring, or of young lives which, from the earliest dawn of infancy, had been one horrible endurance of cruelty and neglect. There were little faces which should have been handsome, darkened with the scowl of sullen, dogged suffering; there was childhood with the light of its eye quenched, its beauty gone, and its helplessness alone remaining; there were vicious-faced boys, brooding, with leaden eyes, like malefactors in a jail; and there were young creatures on whom the sins of their frail parents had descended, weeping even for the mercenary nurses they had known, and lonesome even in their loneliness. With every kindly sympathy and affection blasted in its birth, with every young and healthy feeling flogged and starved down, with every revengeful passion that can fester in swollen hearts, eating its evil way to their core in silence, what an incipient Hell was breeding here!

And yet this scene, painful as it was, had its grotesque features, which, in a less interested observer than Nicholas, might have provoked a smile. Mrs Squeers stood at one of the desks, presiding over an immense basin of brimstone and treacle, of which delicious compound she administered a large instalment to each boy in succession: using for the purpose a common wooden spoon, which might have been originally manufactured for some gigantic top, and which widened every young gentleman's mouth considerably: they being all obliged, under heavy corporal penalties, to take in the whole of the bowl at a gasp. In another corner, huddled together for companionship, were the little boys who had arrived on the preceding night, three of them in very large leather breeches, and two in old trousers, a something tighter fit than drawers are usually worn; at no great distance from these was seated the juvenile son and heir of Mr Squeers – a striking likeness of his father – kicking, with great vigour, under the hands of Smike, who was fitting upon him a pair of new boots that bore a most suspicious resemblance to those which the least of the little boys had worn on the journey down – as the little boy himself seemed to think, for he was regarding the appropriation with a look of most rueful amazement. Besides these, there was a long row of boys waiting, with countenances of no pleasant anticipation, to be treacled; and another file, who had just escaped from the infliction, making a variety of wry mouths indicative of anything but satisfaction. The whole were attired in such motley, ill-assorted, extraordinary garments, as would have been irresistibly ridiculous, but for the foul appearance of dirt, disorder, and disease, with which they were associated.

'Now,' said Squeers, giving the desk a great rap with his cane, which made half the little boys nearly jump out of their boots, 'is that physicking over?'

'Just over,' said Mrs Squeers, choking the last boy in her hurry, and tapping the crown of his head with the wooden spoon to restore him. 'Here, you Smike; take away now. Look sharp!'

Smike shuffled out with the basin, and Mrs Squeers having called up a little boy with a curly head, and wiped her hands upon it, hurried out after him into a species of wash-house, where there was a small fire and a large kettle, together with a number of little wooden bowls which were arranged upon a board.

Into these bowls, Mrs Squeers, assisted by the hungry servant, poured a brown composition, which looked like diluted pincushions without the covers, and was called porridge. A minute wedge of brown bread was inserted in each bowl, and when they had eaten their porridge by means of the bread, the boys ate the bread itself, and had finished their breakfast; whereupon Mr Squeers said, in a solemn voice, 'For what we have received, may the Lord make us truly thankful!' – and went away to his own.

Nicholas distended his stomach with a bowl of porridge, for much the same reason which induces some savages to swallow earth – lest they should be inconveniently hungry when there is nothing to eat. Having further disposed of a slice of bread and butter, allotted to him in virtue of his office, he sat himself down, to wait for school-time.

He could not but observe how silent and sad the boys all seemed to be. There was none of the noise and clamour of a schoolroom; none of its boisterous play, or hearty mirth. The children sat crouching and shivering together, and seemed to lack the spirit to move about. The only pupil who evinced the slightest tendency towards locomotion or playfulness was Master Squeers, and as his chief amusement was to tread upon the other boys' toes in his new boots, his flow of spirits was rather disagreeable than otherwise.

After some half-hour's delay, Mr Squeers reappeared, and the boys took their places and their books, of which latter commodity the average might be about one to eight learners. A few minutes having elapsed, during which Mr Squeers looked very profound, as if he had a perfect apprehension of what was inside all the books, and could say every word of their contents by heart if he only chose to take the trouble, that gentleman called up the first class.

Obedient to this summons there ranged themselves in front of the schoolmaster's desk, half-a-dozen scarecrows, out at knees and elbows, one of whom placed a torn and filthy book beneath his learned eye.

'This is the first class in English spelling and philosophy, Nickleby,' said Squeers, beckoning Nicholas to stand beside him. 'We'll get up a Latin one, and hand that over to you. Now, then, where's the first boy?'

'Please, sir, he's cleaning the back-parlour window,' said the temporary head of the philosophical class.

'So he is, to be sure,' rejoined Squeers. 'We go upon the practical mode of teaching, Nickleby; the regular education system. C-l-e-a-n, clean, verb active, to make bright, to scour. W-i-n, win, d-e-r, der, winder, a casement. When the boy knows this out of book, he goes and does it. It's just the same principle as the use of the globes. Where's the second boy?'

'Please, sir, he's weeding the garden,' replied a small voice.

'To be sure,' said Squeers, by no means disconcerted. 'So he is. B-o-t, bot, t-i-n, tin, bottin, n-e-y, ney, bottinney, noun substantive, a knowledge of plants. When he has learned that bottinney means a knowledge of plants, he goes and knows 'em. That's our system, Nickleby: what do you think of it?'

'It's very useful one, at any rate,' answered Nicholas.

Charles Dickens

UNDERSTANDING THE TEXT

1 How can you tell that the schoolroom is in a bad condition?

2 What is Nicholas's reaction to the sight of his new pupils?

3 How does Mrs Squeers give out the brimstone and treacle?

4 What does she then wipe her hands on?

5 Why is the sound of the classroom so different from what we would expect?

INTERPRETING THE TEXT

6 Why do you think the writer calls the hero by his first name – Nicholas – and the schoolmaster by his last name – Squeers?

7 What clues are there that the text is set in the past?

> **HINTS**
>
> ● Look at things that happen in the story
> ● Look at the characters' use of language

8 What can you tell about Nicholas's attitude to what he sees – is he disapproving or neutral?

9 How does Charles Dickens build our sympathy for the boys at the school, and make us dislike Squeers and his wife?

10 **a** What can you learn from the extract about the way private schools might have been organized and run in Dickens' time?

   b Write a paragraph showing how the school described in the extract is different from the schools you have been in.

LANGUAGE AND STRUCTURE

1 To bring the scene to life, Charles Dickens uses some vivid descriptions, such as this one of the porridge:

a brown composition, which looked like diluted pincushions without the covers

What impression does this image create of the porridge?

2 One feature of Dickens' style is that he often uses very long, complex sentences. He also sometimes uses an elaborate or complicated way of expressing ideas. Look, for example, at this construction:

... the boys took their places and their books, of which latter commodity the average might be about one to eight learners.

How might you say this more simply?

3 Dickens' complex sentences often contain colons or semi-colons between the different phrases. Choose a sentence that includes at least one colon or semi-colon, and describe the job that the punctuation is doing in that sentence.

4 The text was written more than 150 years ago. What clues can you find in the language that hint at its age?

5 Paragraphs 2, 3 and 4 are very long – much longer than you would expect to see in most texts written today. Look at paragraph 4, beginning 'And yet this scene ...' If you had to divide it into shorter paragraphs, which of the sentences would you choose to start new paragraphs with?

6 As well as showing the terrible school conditions, Dickens also includes humour in the scene. He uses irony to hint at what is really going on, such as saying that young Squeers' new boots 'bore a most suspicious resemblance' to those previously seen on a new boy (paragraph 4). In the same paragraph, he uses a made-up word, 'treacled', to sum up what Mrs Squeers has done to the boys.

Choose a phrase or sentence that you find humorous, and explain its effects.

WRITING ACTIVITY

We don't see much of Nicholas's opinion of the school in the extract. Imagine the diary he might write that evening. He uses it to say how sickened he is by a) the school environment and b) the way the boys are treated by the Squeers family.

Write his diary entry for the evening that follows the events in the extract. Include vivid descriptions of the scenes he has witnessed.

EXTENDED WRITING

Below is an extract from the stage version of the Nicholas Nickleby story. Written by playwright David Edgar, it is called *The Life and Adventures of Nicholas Nickleby*. It was first performed by the Royal Shakespeare Company in 1980. Then it was filmed and shown on Channel 4 TV, and made available on video.

This extract shows how the writer, David Edgar, uses a large cast to tell the story. The extract comes from the start of Part II (which lasts in total about 4½ hours).

GLOSSARY

tableau – *a silent group of people arranged to represent a scene*

sequestered – *sheltered, hidden from view*

bereaved – *having had a death in the family*

drudge – *person who does all the hard and unpleasant work*

The Life and Adventures of Nicholas Nickleby

Act One

Scene One

As the audience come in, the Company mingles with them, welcoming them to the show. Eventually, the whole company assembles on stage. A Narrator steps forward, to start the re-cap of the story of Part One. During this Narration, the Company makes small tableaux that reminds us of incidents in Part One.

Narrator: The story so far. There once lived, in a sequestered part of the county of Devonshire,

Mrs Nickleby: A mother,

Kate: And a daughter,

Nicholas: And a son.

Narrator: Who, recently bereaved, were forced to journey up to London, and to throw themselves upon the mercy of their only living relative, Ralph Nickleby.

Ralph: All three of 'em in London, damn 'em,

Noggs: He'd growled to his clerk,

Ralph: And you, sir? You're prepared to work?

Narrator: He'd demanded of his nephew, and receiving the firm answer

Nicholas: Yes!

Narrator: Ralph took young Nicholas and found him a position in a school in Yorkshire run by

Squeers: Mr Wackford Squeers.

Nicholas: Well, thank you, uncle. I will not forget this kindness.

Narrator: And arriving at the school, he met with

Mrs Squeers: Mrs Squeers,

Fanny: Their daughter Fanny,

Young Wackford: Their son young Wackford,

Narrator: And their poor drudge:

Mrs Squeers: Smike!

Narrator: And forty boys, with pale and haggard faces, lank and bony figures, children with the countenances of old men, all darkened with the scowl of sullen, dogged suffering.

Squeers: So – what d'you say?

Boys: For what we have received, may the Lord make us truly thankful.

David Edgar

Speaking and listening

a Start by working in a group to think about how you would present this fast-paced storytelling sequence. How would it work on stage?

Some photographs from the RSC version are included to show how they approached the task.

b Discuss the way the writer compresses the storyline.

c Discuss the way you get a glimpse of different characters.

d Think about ways of making this sequence exciting to an audience who do not know anything about Charles Dickens.

Writing

1 Write about the ways in which the stage version feels different from the novel. You might comment on:

♦ the pace of the story

♦ the level of detail you get about characters and themes

♦ how far the writer has used similar language.

2 How do you think the text would work on stage? Write a description of the way you would present it if you were the director. How would you keep it moving quickly? How would you show the change of scenes?

12

Multiple narration

Introduction

Stories are often structured so that they have more than one storyline. Think of films and television dramas; in most soap operas the average length of a scene will be less than 15 seconds, then we will switch to different characters in a different setting. In this way, the writer can push the story forward by constantly moving between different groups of characters.

Fiction writers often use this technique, especially when they wish to build suspense. The key moments of the novel *Jaws*, for example, switch rapidly between the 'big fish' out at sea and the victim swimming in the water.

One paragraph focuses on the shark, the next on the boy, then the shark again, as the writer gradually draws the two storylines together. This is known as **multiple narration**.

This unit looks at a complete short story, which is told through the use of two narratives. Elizabeth Garner's story is confusing at first and difficult to follow. She makes the reader work hard to follow what is being described. Suddenly it becomes clearer, once we understand how the two storylines connect.

A Lesson

> ### OBJECTIVES
>
> These are the objectives you will be studying:
>
> - Word level: *layers of meaning*
> - Sentence level: *paragraph organization*
> - Reading: *rhetorical devices*
> - Writing: *narrative techniques*, and *cite textual evidence*
> - Speaking and listening: *compare points of view*, and (arrive at a) *considered viewpoint*

A Lesson

He was trying to teach them Geography — or so he said. He drew on the globe a black dot. It marked a town in Australia.

The town on the other side of the world plunged into darkness. No match would strike. No fire could burn. In terrified blindness they all reached for the modern reassurance of electricity. The switches gave nothing. Together they rushed to their television sets and turned them on.

Blank.

There was nothing; not even a dancing fog of black and white dots. Only a silent, menacing darkness.

They tried to tune their radios to hear some sound other than their own.

Silence.

The speakers hissed at them.

They thought that it was the end of the world.

He was trying to teach them Geography — or so he said. He spun the globe faster and faster.

Words which marked time were soon forgotten. Lifetimes dwindled to a passing moment.

Their suffering did not last long. They became accustomed to the dark silence which grew over them. They each held their own dark close.

He stopped the globe.

Time waited for him.

He wiped the black dot clean and placed the globe on the table.

On the other side of the world the sun shone through the town. The radios spewed loud music. Brightly-coloured figures leered at them from their television screens. These sudden noises attacked them all. They felt it was the end of their world.

He looked up and saw that the classroom was empty. He thought it was some childish prank. He stood up sharply, in his anger knocking over the globe. It fell and shattered into a thousand pieces.

Elizabeth Garner

UNDERSTANDING THE TEXT

1 What does the teacher do?

2 What is the effect of his action?

3 How do the people on the other side of the world react?

4 Why does the teacher get angry at the end of the story?

INTERPRETING THE TEXT

5 What impression do you get of the teacher in the story? What hints are there that he is not entirely good or trustworthy?

6 How does the writer make the people seem helpless and panicky?

7 How can you tell that there is a link between what the teacher does and what happens across the world?

8 What do you think is the writer's 'message' in the story?

- Is she suggesting something about the link between what we do on this side of the world and its impact elsewhere?

- Is she showing us someone who is evil?

- Is she simply writing a supernatural story?

Explain your ideas.

9 Why do you think the story is called 'A Lesson'?

LANGUAGE AND STRUCTURE

1 a One rhetorical device in this story is the author's use of pronouns. Look at the first paragraph. The writer refers to the teacher as 'he' rather than giving him a name. What effect does this have?

b Look at the second paragraph. Why does the writer call the people 'they' and avoid giving names, or any descriptive detail?

2 The writer sometimes uses very short paragraphs, like this:

Blank.

Silence.

Why do you think she structures them like this?

3 The writer uses a dual narrative to tell her story. Why do you think she does this? Write a couple of sentences to explain how the dual narrative increases the tension in the story.

4 Read this comment on the story:

The writer makes us dislike the teacher. She wants us to feel that he is untrustworthy, even evil.

In a small group, discuss whether you agree with this statement. What evidence can you find in the story to support it? Try to reach agreement in your group. Make notes of your findings and your evidence, and report back to the class.

WRITING ACTIVITY

How could you make the teacher in the opening paragraph a more sympathetic (likeable) character? Would it have an impact if he:

◆ was given a name?

◆ was described in greater detail?

◆ was given some dialogue?

Try writing an opening paragraph in which you aim to show that the teacher is a trustworthy, likeable character who is simply doing his job.

You might start like this:

'Morning everyone,' said Mr …

Then write a paragraph explaining how you approached the task.

EXTENDED WRITING

Here is the outline of a story:

A child is digging in the garden. Suddenly the child finds something he or she doesn't recognize. The child digs harder, and then looks closely – it's flesh of some kind, grey and thick. Suddenly it moves. The earth starts to shift. A baby dinosaur starts to scramble out of the earth. The child is first terrified, and then delighted.

Try writing the opening paragraphs of this story using the narrative devices below:

A	B	C
Open the story with the child digging. Tell the story in chronological order. Tell it in the third person ('he' or 'she')	Open the story with the leg moving, and something pushing through the soil. Cut to the child's mother watching from the kitchen window. She sees something is going on and rushes out. Cut to the child, panic stricken. Cut to the mother running out to help.	Open with the dinosaur lying beneath the earth. Tell the story from the dinosaur's point of view, like this: 'I had lain there, beneath that dusty soil, for as long as I could remember …' Then cut to the child on the surface just about to start digging.

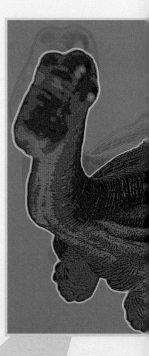

When you have finished, decide which version works best. Write a few sentences to explain why.

Conveying ideas

Introduction

Non-fiction writers sometimes use the techniques we expect of poets and novelists. They might use figurative language (e.g. similes, metaphors and personification), or sentence structure to capture our attention.

In this unit you will compare two non-fiction texts. The first text is an example of sports writing, and it combines autobiography with storytelling. It describes Andy Martin's first time surfing on a fashionable Quigly surfboard. The second text is from a website belonging to the University of San Diego, California. It gives hints on surfing.

Comparing the two texts should help you to see the difference between literary non-fiction and straight non-fiction writing.

Walking on Water

OBJECTIVES

You will be studying the following objectives:

- Word level: *layers of meaning*
- Sentence level: *degrees of formality*, and *conventions of ICT texts*
- Reading: *information retrieval, compare texts, interpretation of text*, and *rhetorical devices*
- Writing: *creativity in non-literary texts*, 'infotainment' (how information texts can be amusing and entertaining), and *integrate information*

Text A

The writer, Andy Martin, has lent a pair of eye-catching socks to his friend, Louis. In return, he gets to borrow Louis's state-of-the-art surfboard …

Walking on Water

Louis had a beautiful board. It was a remake of a classic 60s malibu: nine feet long, broad in the hip, but light, with a rounded nose and three fins, in deep blue with orange stripes and a crimson rim. It bore the signature of Quigly, a West Coast shaper who had been prominent in the revival of the longboard in the eighties.

I lusted after that Quigly. Thus it was that when Louis wondered if there was anything he could do for me in return for the socks, I mentioned I was currently without a board.

'You want to borrow my Quigly?' he said. It was more a plea than a question. Unscrambled, his message read: 'Please don't take my Quigly! It's the love of my life.'

I was implacable. 'If you can spare it for a few hours,' I said.

'Have you surfed much on the North Shore?' he inquired.

'Sure,' I said, truthfully. 'Jocko's, Freddie's, Haleiwa, Lani's, Backyards. All over.' I passed over the details of what had taken place.

'Oh well, I guess that's all right, then.' He sounded reassured.

The following morning I steered the Quigly into the car like a kidnap victim and headed for Haleiwa. Bodo and Damon were waiting for me.

'That's a fine board you have there,' said Bodo.

'A Quigly,' I boasted.

'Wow!' gasped Damon. 'They're like gold dust in California.'

I had a good feeling about that board. It felt right as I gave it a solid basting of wax and uncurled the leash, and it felt right as I paddled it out: well balanced, smooth through the water, responsive. Bodo called it a 'modern tanker': it was a subtle compromise between a gondola and a toothpick, combining the virtues of robustness and sensitivity, stability and speed.

I followed Bodo and Damon out through the channel. The Quigly sliced through the oncoming waves like a knife through butter, so by the time we hit the line-up I was still in good shape. There was a right-hander and further over towards the harbour a left. We opted for the left, which was less crowded. Bodo and Damon drove straight at the peak. But I didn't want to push my luck and followed my usual cautious procedure of testing out the unoccupied shoulder.

I lined myself up with an easygoing four- to five-footer as it ambled into shore, despised by the hunters further out who were stalking bigger game. I got into gear and rammed the Quigly ahead of the swell. Then I felt the wave hook itself under the rear and start to jack it up. I cranked out another couple of strokes and leapt to my feet.

It was almost too easy. It was like riding a bicycle successfully for the first time: you can't understand why you had so much difficulty before, just as before it was impossible to understand how the deed could ever be done. My feet were planted in the textbook position: my left foot halfway up the board, sideways on but angled towards the nose, my right foot slanted across the board at the tail. Surprised to find myself still upright, I flung out my arms and crouched, modelling myself on the famous picture of Eddie Aikau. The Quigly planed down the face and, almost without my exerting any effort, began to curve into a leisurely bottom turn. Behind me and to the right, the wave was bursting apart: over my left shoulder was an unbroken section. I leaned over, slid my weight onto my right foot, and the Quigly carved a voluptuous line along the crystal-blue wall, like Michelangelo shaping his Madonna. I had no idea how long I'd been standing up. Chronometrically, it would be insignificant; but I have a mental clock permanently arrested with its hands on that morning and that wave. 'No one times how long the ride is,' Mark Foo had said to me. 'It's so intense, the duration doesn't matter. A second is a long time on the wave.'

Andy Martin

Text B

http://et.sdsu.edu/theffernan/surfing/judging.htm

Home My Netscape

Judging Waves

Bigger isn't better for beginners. Waves can pack quite a wallop. And a loose board driven by a large wave becomes a missile.

Take it from me, getting slammed to the bottom by a big wave is no fun.

You don't need a 'perfect wave' to learn how to surf. Most people earn their sea legs in the white water or 'soup' that results from a breaking wave.

Getting your balance for the first time on a pitching plank will be hard enough (and exciting enough) even in the soup.

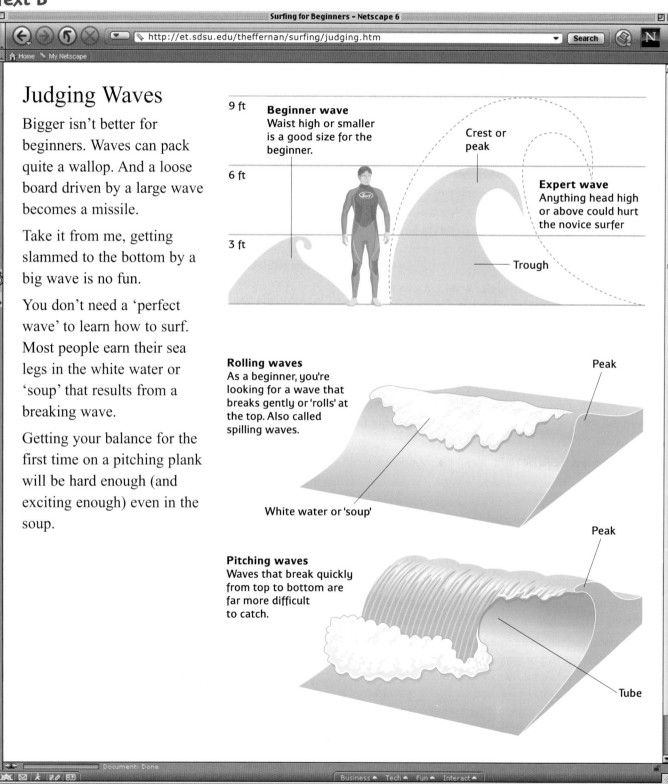

9 ft

6 ft

3 ft

Beginner wave
Waist high or smaller is a good size for the beginner.

Crest or peak

Expert wave
Anything head high or above could hurt the novice surfer

Trough

Rolling waves
As a beginner, you're looking for a wave that breaks gently or 'rolls' at the top. Also called spilling waves.

Peak

White water or 'soup'

Pitching waves
Waves that break quickly from top to bottom are far more difficult to catch.

Peak

Tube

Document: Done

Business   Tech   Fun   Interact

http://et.sdsu.edu/theffernan/surfing/tip_sheet.htm ▾ Search

Home My Netscape

Beginner's Tip Sheet

To help remember what you need to do when that awesome wave is coming, print out this page. Next, trim it with scissors to match the nose of your surfboard, then tape it down with two-inch-wide clear packing tape. Be sure to cover the entire paper with tape. Now, let's go surfing!

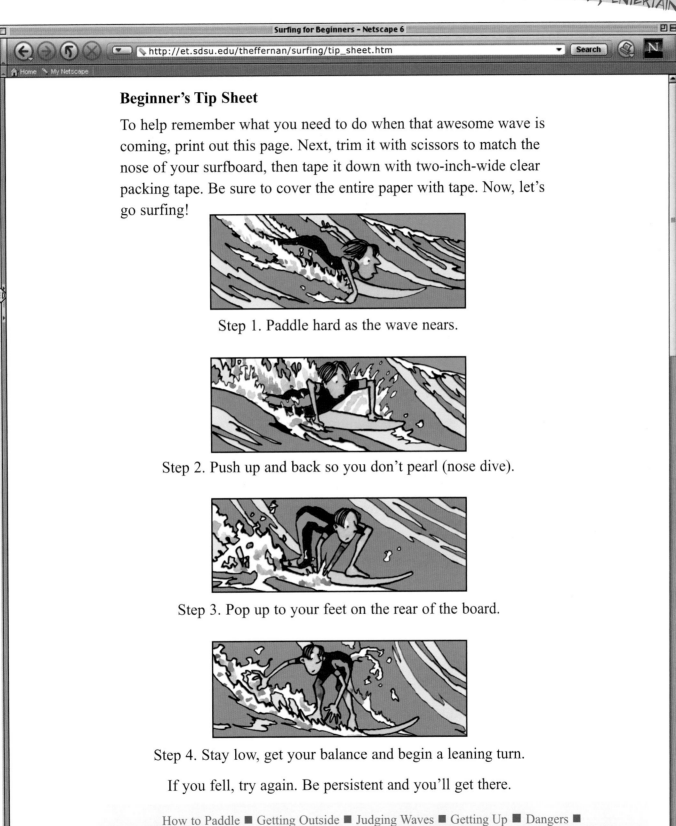

Step 1. Paddle hard as the wave nears.

Step 2. Push up and back so you don't pearl (nose dive).

Step 3. Pop up to your feet on the rear of the board.

Step 4. Stay low, get your balance and begin a leaning turn.

If you fell, try again. Be persistent and you'll get there.

How to Paddle ■ Getting Outside ■ Judging Waves ■ Getting Up ■ Dangers ■ Some Rules ■ Exercise ■ Equipment ■ Tip Sheet ■ Credits ■ Lessons ■ Vacations ■ Home Page

Document: Done

Business▲ Tech▲ Fun▲ Interact▲

UNDERSTANDING THE TEXT

Text A

1 Why is the surfboard called a Quigly?

2 Does Louis really want the narrator to borrow his board? How can you tell?

3 How does the writer get the board ready before going out to sea?

4 How can you tell that the Quigly performs well in the water?

5 What point does the writer make about time at the end of the extract?

Text B

6 In surfing, what does the word 'soup' mean?

7 What is another term for rolling waves?

8 Name two dangers for beginners that the writer mentions.

INTERPRETING THE TEXT

Text A

9 How does the writer make the Quigly surfboard seem glamorous and exciting?

> **HINTS**
>
> Look at:
>
> - the way he describes it
> - how other people react to it
> - the writer's own feelings about it

10 How can you tell that the new surfboard makes surfing easier than the writer expected?

Text B

11 How does the writer reassure readers that, with practice, they will become successful surfers?

12 a How useful do you find the diagrams in this text? Do they help explain how to surf? Are they more or less informative than the words beside them?

b Write a sentence or two to describe the ways you extracted information from this text to answer the questions – did the diagrams and labels help you?

13 This text comes from a website. How would you know that if you had not been told? Are there any clues in the text that show it is from the Internet?

Comparison

14 How would you describe the purpose and audience of the two texts?

15 Which text makes surfing seem more exciting? Explain why.

LANGUAGE AND STRUCTURE

Text A

1 In the first paragraph, the writer describes the Quigly surfboard as having a 'hip', a 'nose', and 'fins'. What is the effect of this use of familiar words?

2 One rhetorical device the writer uses is vivid figurative language. Say in your own words what you think he means in each of these sentences:

a *It was a subtle compromise between a gondola and a toothpick.*

b *The Quigly carved a voluptuous line along the crystal-blue wall, like Michelangelo shaping his Madonna.*

c *I have a mental clock permanently arrested with its hands on that morning and that wave.*

3 Look at another of his descriptions using figurative language:

I lined myself up with an easygoing four- to five-footer as it ambled into shore, despised by the hunters further out who were stalking bigger game.

a What is he referring to when he says:

  i *four- to five-footer*

  ii *the hunters further out*

  iii *bigger game?*

b The language here uses metaphor, comparing one object with another to help the reader visualize it. How does the choice of metaphor capture the excitement of the waves?

Text B

4 Look at the first paragraph of the text. The writer says: 'Waves can pack quite a wallop'. If the text were written in a more formal way, how might the writer have expressed the same idea?

5 The writer's next sentence begins with 'And'. Many writers avoid starting with a conjunction like this. Why do you think this writer does so?

6 The writer uses the second-person form to address the reader directly – for example:

You don't need a 'perfect wave' …
Getting your balance for the first time …

How do you, as a reader, react to the writer? Does he seem:

expert   arrogant   reassuring   helpful   big-headed   self-confident enthusiastic?

Choose the one word which you think best describes his tone. Explain your response with examples from the text.

WRITING ACTIVITY

Text A captures the excitement of surfing using vivid language. How would a more factual report present the same material?

Write a one-paragraph factual report of Andy Martin's experience, to appear in a local newspaper or magazine. Simply give the facts about the board he is using, and how he rides the board. Write it in the third person:

Andy Martin borrowed a Quigly surfboard from …

UNIT 13

EXTENDED WRITING

The Internet is a means of giving information to readers in an entertaining, interactive way. Web pages can use text and images, plus music, animations and video.

Choose a topic you know a lot about. Some possibilities are given below. Then design a website which combines information with entertainment.

Think about how you can make the information as attractive and useful as possible. Think also about your audience. How will you choose your language and layout?

You might:

◆ use short blocks of text

◆ use subheadings and bullet points to make text clearer

◆ build in an interactive quiz

◆ include hyperlinks to other pages

◆ use images and animations.

Possible topics

◆ How to skateboard

◆ How to download an MP3 file

◆ How to make the tastiest sandwich

◆ How to edit a digital movie

◆ How to improve the look of a word-processed document (using font styles, sizes, bold, underline, etc.)

Remember that the aim is to communicate information in an entertaining way.

Use a sheet of A4 paper to draft the website. For images, animations, and movies, simply label them on the page (you don't have to draw them).

UNIT 13

Speaking and listening
Special assignment

OBJECTIVES

This special assignment gives you the chance to practise interviewing. These are the objectives you will be studying:

● Speaking: *evaluate own talk*, and *interview techniques*

● Listening: *evaluate own listening skills*

Imagine a TV or radio reporter interviews Andy Martin about his first ride on the Quigly. What would the reporter ask? What kind of questions would draw the best answers from Andy Martin? How could the reporter avoid questions which lead to yes/no responses?

Think about your interview questions and then, in pairs, hold a two-minute interview. Swap roles, and do the interview again.

When you have finished, write a few sentences to describe what you have learnt about interviewing. Which speaking and listening skills do you need to improve for future interview sessions?

Nineteenth-century poetry

Introduction

As we saw in Unit 10, poetry comes in a variety of forms and styles. This unit looks at two writers, one from America who wrote in the 1800s; the other from Ireland who is one of the world's most admired poets today. The two poets are Emily Dickinson and Seamus Heaney.

Emily Dickinson is one of America's most amazing poets. Born in 1830, she spent most of the later years of her life confined to her home – refusing to leave the house. She wrote and wrote, producing around 2000 poems, and yet only around seven of them were published while she was alive, and they were considered deeply odd.

Her poems describe her thoughts and feelings, often about love, death and religion. She has a very individual style, and it upset some of her early readers. For example, she used punctuation in an unexpected way, as you will see when you look at one of her poems.

One of Emily Dickinson's poems is presented here in two different versions. The first is the original version, with the punctuation as Emily Dickinson intended it. The second is a modern, edited version which aims to standardize her punctuation to make it less 'wacky'. See how the different versions read.

The poem is on one of Emily Dickinson's constant themes. She describes the effects of a death which has happened across the street.

There's Been a Death

GLOSSARY

milliner – *person who makes or sells hats*

intuition – *impression*

Version A

There's been a Death, in the Opposite House,
As lately as Today –
I know it, by the numb look
Such Houses have – alway –

The Neighbours rustle in and out –
The Doctor – drives away –
A Window opens like a Pod –
Abrupt – mechanically –

Somebody flings a Mattress out –
The Children hurry by –
They wonder if it died – on that –
I used to – when a Boy –

The Minister – goes stiffly in –
As if the House were His –
And He owned all the Mourners – now –
And little Boys – besides –

And then the Milliner – and the Man
Of the Appalling Trade –
To take the measure of the House –
There'll be that Dark Parade –

Of Tassels – and of Coaches – soon –
It's easy as a Sign –
The Intuition of the News –
In just a Country Town –

Version B

There's been a death in the opposite house
As lately as today.
I know it by the numb look
Such houses have alway.

The neighbours rustle in and out;
The doctor drives away.
A window opens like a pod,
Abrupt, mechanically;

Somebody flings a mattress out.
The children hurry by;
They wonder if it died on that.
I used to, when a boy.

The minister goes stiffly in
As if the house were his
And he owned all the mourners now,
And little boys besides;

And then the milliner, and the man
Of the appalling trade
To take the measure of the house.
There'll be that dark parade

Of tassels and of coaches soon.
It's easy as a sign –
The intuition of the news
In just a country town.

Emily Dickinson

UNDERSTANDING THE TEXT

1 Look at the first stanza of versions A and B. Write down two differences you notice in their layout.

2 Following the death at the house, a number of people visit. Write down three people or groups who call.

3 Why are the children curious about the mattress?

4 Who do you think is the 'man of the appalling trade'?

5 What clue is there in line 12 that this poem is not based on Emily Dickinson's own life?

INTERPRETING THE TEXT

6 How does the narrator know that there has been a death?

7 What impression does the verb 'rustle' give of the neighbours?

8 What impression does the adverb 'stiffly' give of the minister?

9 What do you think the message of the poem is overall? Choose the statement you most agree with, or write your own different statement. Then write a sentence to explain your choice.

   a People always react in the same way to death.

   b People aren't really themselves after a death.

   c People are very formal following a death.

   d No one really cares about the family following a death.

10 What impression do you get of the narrator of the poem?

> HINTS
>
> - Look at his attitude to what he sees
> - Think about whether he gets involved
> - Look at the way he describes people and events

LANGUAGE AND STRUCTURE

1 Version A uses capital letters and punctuation very differently from version B.

  a Read each version of the poem aloud. Do you read them differently because of the different punctuation? In what way?

  b How does the different punctuation change the meaning of the poem?

2 Look at the way the writer uses rhythm and rhyme in the poem.

  a Is it regular all the way through?

  b How do the rhythm and rhyme add to the effect of the poem? Do they make the subject seem more serious, or less?

3 How would you describe the tone of the poem (the writer's attitude to the subject)? Choose one of the words below, or give your own:

serious sombre fascinated horrified neutral curious

Explain your choice.

4 What clues are there in the language that the poem is set in a different period?

WRITING ACTIVITY

The poem describes the narrator's observations of people's reaction to a death in a small town. Rewrite the description to show how it would sound in prose rather than poetry – for example as a diary entry or a description at the start of a novel. Use standard English to describe the scene, and try to make your writing rich in detailed description.

What is gained or lost by presenting the material in this way? Write a paragraph comparing the effect of your work to that of the poem.

UNIT 14

Twentieth-century poetry

Introduction

Seamus Heaney was born in 1939 and grew up in the countryside of Northern Ireland. He wrote about this in much of his early poetry, sometimes writing about his own family, and also reflecting on the political 'Troubles' of Ireland which have led to conflict and violence over hundreds of years.

This poem is a personal one and, like Emily Dickinson's poem on pages 106–107, it describes the writer's feelings following a death. The death is of the narrator's brother.

Mid-term Break

OBJECTIVES

These are the objectives you will be studying:

- Word level: *layers of meaning*, and *connectives for developing thought*
- Reading: *evaluate own critical writing*, and *rhetorical devices*
- Writing: *balanced analysis*, and *cite textual evidence*
- Speaking and listening: *compare points of view*, and *(arrive at a) considered viewpoint*

GLOSSARY

knelling – *tolling (a death knell is a bell used at funerals)*

stanched – *the blood flow stopped*

Mid-term Break

I sat all morning in the college sick bay
Counting bells knelling classes to a close.
At two o'clock our neighbours drove me home.

In the porch I met my father crying –
He had always taken funerals in his stride –
And Big Jim Evans saying it was a hard blow.

The baby cooed and laughed and rocked the pram
When I came in, and I was embarrassed
By old men standing up to shake my hand

And tell me they were 'sorry for my trouble';
Whispers informed strangers I was the eldest,
Away at school, as my mother held my hand

In hers and coughed out angry tearless sighs.
At ten o'clock the ambulance arrived
With the corpse, stanched and bandaged by the nurses.

Next morning I went up into the room. Snowdrops
And candles soothed the bedside; I saw him
For the first time in six weeks. Paler now,

Wearing a poppy bruise on his left temple,
He lay in the four foot box as in his cot.
No gaudy scars, the bumper knocked him clear.

A four foot box, a foot for every year.

Seamus Heaney

UNDERSTANDING THE TEXT

1 Why does the narrator spend the morning in the sick bay? Is it because he is ill?

2 How do people first react when the narrator arrives home?

3 When he gets home, his house is full of sadness, except for the baby. What does the baby do?

4 How did his brother die?

5 How old was he when he died?

INTERPRETING THE TEXT

6 What do you learn about the narrator from the poem? How does he feel about what is going on?

7 In the room with his dead brother, there are snowdrops. Why do you think Seamus Heaney has included this detail about the type of flowers?

8 Look at these two statements:

  a The narrator is very emotional.

  b The narrator shows no emotion.

Write down which statement you most agree with, and say why.

LANGUAGE AND STRUCTURE

1 This text is set out in short lines like a poem, but are there any other language features that make it seem like poetry? Look for word patterns, rhythm and rhyme. Write a short paragraph saying what other evidence there is that this is a poem.

2 Look more closely at stanzas 1 and 2.

  a How can you tell that this is set in the writer's childhood?

  b How does the writer tell us that the section starting 'In the porch' happens a bit later than the first?

3 From stanzas 2 to 6, write down three words or phrases the writer uses as connectives to show that time has moved forward.

4 Look at the section from stanza 2 to the first line of stanza 5. Here, the writer uses quite long sentences. The poem then ends with much shorter sentences. What effect does this contrast in sentence types have? How does it add to the emotional impact of the poem?

5 The writer gives us information later in the poem that helps the reader to understand what happened earlier.

  a Find an example of this.

  b Explain why you think the writer uses this technique.

6 In pairs or a small group, discuss:

- how the writer creates a picture of his home and family
- how he builds emotion into the poem
- how the subject would have been presented differently if it was part of an autobiography or story, rather than a poem
- parts of the poem you particularly like or dislike.

WRITING ACTIVITY

1 After the discussion in question 6 above, write about your views of the poem. Remember to quote words and lines to support your argument. In particular, explain how the subject matter might have been presented differently if it was part of an autobiography or story, rather than a poem.

2 When you have finished, write an evaluation of your work on the poem. What have you done well, and which skills do you need to develop further for writing about poetry?

Unit 14

EXTENDED WRITING

1 Look at the way Emily Dickinson writes in short, disjointed units of meaning, punctuated by dashes. Compare this with Seamus Heaney's more conversational style of storytelling to recount a memory from his childhood. Which style do you feel is more successful here, and why?

2 Choose a difficult or troubling experience from your life. Some examples are given below.

   ◆ a time you got into trouble

   ◆ the death of a pet

   ◆ suddenly being afraid that there was an intruder in your house

   ◆ being afraid of going to school

   ◆ learning to swim or ride a bike.

Try to write a short, powerful poem about the memory of this experience. Write about what happened and how it affected you. Spend time deciding on just the right words and images. Make your language compressed by cutting out any unnecessary words.

You might try to use the style of Emily Dickinson or Seamus Heaney, or your own preferred style. Use rhyme and rhythm if appropriate.

Your main aim should be to write something which captures and communicates the experience in an appropriate way.

3 Write a paragraph commenting upon your poem. What language decisions did you make? How did you change things after the first draft? Which parts of the poem do you think work especially well? Which are you less happy with?

Thriller writing

Introduction

When we read modern writers it can be easy to forget that they are often part of a tradition of writing. A novelist writing today may use techniques of characterization and plotting first used by a much earlier writer, such as Charles Dickens or Jane Austen.

The *Harry Potter* books, for example, have echoes of Charles Dickens' techniques in their memorable names and quirky characters. David Almond's novels such as *Skellig* and *Kit's Wilderness* have the clear, pure writing style of storytellers like Raymond Carver.

This unit is about tradition and influence, and the way the influence of one writer's work may emerge in the writing of a much later author. The main focus of the unit is on detective and mystery writing.

In the late nineteenth century, readers became intrigued by mystery stories. Charles Dickens had himself written an unfinished thriller called *The Mystery of Edwin Drood*. Other writers at the time created novels like *The Woman in White* by Wilkie Collins and *Dr Jekyll and Mr Hyde* by Robert Louis Stevenson (you can read an extract from this on page 39–40).

It was also the period when Sherlock Holmes was invented by Sir Arthur Conan Doyle, and this led to a tradition of famous detectives in the writing of people like Georges Simenon, Dorothy L. Sayers, Agatha Christie, Raymond Chandler, Dashiell Hammett, Ruth Rendell, P.D. James and Patricia Cornwell.

In this unit we compare two thriller writers – one from the nineteenth century, the other from the twentieth: Edgar Allan Poe and Len Deighton.

On a Mission

OBJECTIVES

These are the objectives you will be studying:

- Word level: *layers of meaning*
- Sentence level: *integrate speech, reference and quotation*, and *trends over time*
- Reading: *compare texts, compare writers from different times, rhetorical devices*, and *major writers*
- Writing: *narrative techniques*

Edgar Allan Poe is sometimes described as the creator of the detective story. He loved to create tales of horror and evil, as well as stories in which the reader had to try to guess – through the eyes of the expert detective – who the murderer might be. This was the beginning of the 'whodunnit'. This extract from his short story The Tell Tale Heart shows the mind of a murderer as he kills an old man by scaring him to death.

Text A

GLOSSARY

death watches – *beetles which live in old wood, and make a ticking sound*

suppositions – *ideas*

waned – *wore out*

scantlings – *small wooden cross-beams*

The Tell Tale Heart

His room was as black as pitch with the thick darkness (for the shutters were close fastened through fear of robbers), and so I knew that he could not see the opening of the door, and I kept pushing it on steadily, steadily.

I had my head in, and was about to open the lantern, when my thumb slipped upon the tin fastening, and the old man sprang up in the bed, crying out, 'Who's there?'

I kept quite still and said nothing. For a whole hour I

did not move a muscle, and in the meantime I did not hear him lie down. He was still sitting up in the bed, listening; just as I have done night after night hearkening to the death watches in the wall.

Presently, I heard a slight groan, and I knew it was the groan of mortal terror. It was not a groan of pain or of grief – oh, no! It was the low stifled sound that arises from the bottom of the soul when overcharged with awe. I knew the sound well. Many a night, just at midnight, when all the world slept, it has welled up from my own bosom, deepening, with its dreadful echo, the terrors that distracted me. I say I knew it well. I knew what the old man felt, and pitied him although I chuckled at heart. I knew that he had been lying awake ever since the first slight noise when he had turned in the bed. His fears had been ever since growing upon him. He had been trying to fancy them causeless, but could not. He had been saying to himself, 'It is nothing but the wind in the chimney, it is only a mouse crossing the floor,' or, 'It is merely a cricket which has made a single chirp.' Yes, he had been trying to comfort himself with these suppositions; but he had found all in vain. ALL IN VAIN, because Death, in approaching him, had stalked with his black shadow before him and enveloped the victim. And it was the mournful influence of the unperceived shadow that caused him to feel, although he neither saw nor heard, to feel the presence of my head within the room.

When I had waited a long time very patiently without hearing him lie down, I resolved to open a little – a very, very little crevice in the lantern. So I opened it – you cannot imagine how stealthily, stealthily – until at length a single dim ray like the thread of the spider shot out from the crevice and fell upon the vulture eye.

It was open, wide, wide open, and I grew furious as I gazed upon it. I saw it with perfect distinctness – all a dull blue with a hideous veil over it that chilled the very marrow in my bones, but I could see nothing else of the old man's face or person, for I had directed the ray as if by instinct precisely upon the damned spot.

And now, have I not told you that what you mistake for madness is but over-acuteness of the senses? Now, I say, there came to my ears a low, dull, quick sound, such as a watch makes when enveloped in cotton. I knew that sound well too. It was the beating of the old man's heart. It increased my fury as the beating of a drum stimulates the soldier into courage.

But even yet I refrained and kept still. I scarcely breathed. I held the lantern motionless. I tried how steadily I could maintain the ray upon the eye. Meantime the hellish tattoo of the heart increased. It grew quicker and quicker, and louder and louder, every instant. The old man's terror must have been extreme! It grew louder, I say, louder every moment! –

do you mark me well? I have told you that I am nervous: so I am. And now at the dead hour of the night, amid the dreadful silence of that old house, so strange a noise as this excited me to uncontrollable terror. Yet, for some minutes longer I refrained and stood still. But the beating grew louder, louder! I thought the heart must burst. And now a new anxiety seized me – the sound would be heard by a neighbour! The old man's hour had come! With a loud yell, I threw open the lantern and leaped into the room. He shrieked once – once only. In an instant I dragged him to the floor, and pulled the heavy bed over him. I then smiled gaily, to find the deed so far done. But for many minutes the heart beat on with a muffled sound. This, however, did not vex me; it would not be heard through the wall. At length it ceased. The old man was dead. I removed the bed and examined the corpse. Yes, he was stone, stone dead. I placed my hand upon the heart and held it there many minutes. There was no pulsation. He was stone dead. His eye would trouble me no more.

If still you think me mad, you will think so no longer when I describe the wise precautions I took for the concealment of the body. The night waned, and I worked hastily, but in silence.

I took up three planks from the flooring of the chamber, and deposited all between the scantlings. I then replaced the boards so cleverly, so cunningly, that no human eye - not even his - could have detected anything wrong. There was nothing to wash out - no stain of any kind - no blood-spot whatever. I had been too wary for that.

Edgar Allan Poe

Text B

Len Deighton is a master of action novels, often set in a context of war or crime. Novels like this use a mix of plot, description and dialogue to keep up the pace. His writing uses many techniques for building suspense that can be traced back to writers such as Edgar Allan Poe. In this extract an experienced soldier reflects upon a nervous young soldier.

GLOSSARY

demented – *mad*

paraphernalia – *bits and pieces*

subordinates – *people he commands*

profiteer – *someone selling goods for large profits*

prevailed – *went on*

sedition – *treason*

CO – *commanding officer*

Mission Control: Hannibal One

All night I had been inside my headquarters, listening to the wind playing demented tunes upon the army badges, eagles and other paraphernalia that a publicity-conscious army commander had provided to mark the progress of our tiny expedition. I dressed myself in my heavy clothing before venturing outside. The wind blew with renewed violence as I emerged through the shelter's small flap. Each gust crooned a low warning that seemed to vibrate the whole planet before becoming the shrill complaining shriek that penetrated to the centre of my brain. It was a feat of willpower to think clearly. But I was the Mission Commander; unless I was able to think clearly, we might all die.

Others had been here, but only for a few hours at a time. We were the first soldiers to come, and now it looked as if we would be the first men to wage war here. It was a terrible place to fight a battle; a fatal place to lose it. It was a bleak, barren, metallic landscape like none other I had ever seen. I looked up through the clear air, and recognized the constellation of Pleiades, now setting. The neighbouring stars were growing dim. I remembered how as a child I had dreamed of travelling to them.

My second-in-command was an engineer. He was a balding veteran of many years. A fierce disciplinarian with his subordinates, even I was not immune from his sarcastic jeers about youth and inexperience. Perhaps that's why one of the southerners dealing out the rations that day decided to complain directly to me.

'This clothing isn't warm enough, sir. I didn't know it would be as cold as this.'

'You're wearing the same as the others,' I said. 'You'd be no use to the army in a cocoon.'

'It's such a poor-quality material the cold wind goes right through it,' he said, examining his white tunic with finger and thumb. 'A profiteer with an army contract and friends in the Senate doesn't have to worry about how cold we feel.'

'That's all, soldier,' I told him. I wasn't going to let these 'boots' think that the informality that prevailed on these missions extended to the privilege of sedition. 'You volunteered for the trip and your application was endorsed by your CO and agreed by me. Did we all make a mistake about you, soldier?'

'No, sir,' he yelled. 'It's just that where I come from in the south,' he smiled, because his accent made the

qualification unnecessary, 'we never knew temperatures like this.'

I looked at him. He was a weak-faced kid. He'd cut himself shaving, and a spider of dried blood crawled down his jawline. He was probably a good enough soldier left to do a soldier's job, but here he felt inadequate, and those were the ones who showed fear first.

'I'm not looking forward to the trip back, sir. And now the men say there will be fighting before we return.'

There had been mistakes and emergencies during the ascent. The boy needed reassurance. 'It's a routine mission. It was a thousand-to-one chance that they would have men up here, too.' It was a lie, but it seemed to do the trick for him.

'There's no doubt about them being here, then?'

'They're not local inhabitants, if that's what you mean,' I said rather brutally. I spoke too loud, I suppose. My second-in-command heard me and chortled. He looked forward to the fighting. For two decades he'd been in every war the army had fought and he knew that it was the quickest way to promotion. I kept my eyes on the youngster. 'Our mission is reconnaissance, but if they come into this area we will oppose their transit. If that means fighting, we fight.' I saw my Second nod. He turned towards us; he couldn't keep out of a conversation like this. He prodded the boy with enough force to make him wince.

'If you don't like it up here, go home,' he jeered.

Len Deighton

UNDERSTANDING THE TEXT

Text A

1 How can you tell from the start of the extract that the old man is nervous?

2 When the narrator hears the old man's groan, what does it remind him of?

3 When the narrator first notices the beating of the old man's heart, what effect does it have on him?

Text B

4 Look at the first paragraph. How can you tell that it is cold?

5 Why does the narrator feel a strong sense of responsibility?

6 Look at the second paragraph. Where do you think the story is set?

7 Why does the young soldier complain to the narrator rather than the second-in-command?

8 What clues are there that this is a very dangerous mission?

INTERPRETING THE TEXT

Text A

9 What impression do you get of the setting of the story? Where does it take place? What clues are there that it is an old story?

Text B

10 One reader might say: 'The story is set on a distant planet'. Another might say: 'The setting is on Earth, but the landscape is described in this way to show how harsh it is'. Which interpretation do you agree with? Using evidence from the text, explain why.

Comparison

11 What impression do you get of the two narrators? Choose **two** words or phrases (one for each narrator) that you think best sum them up:

tough   heartless   evil   menacing   mad   soft at heart   aggressive   compassionate   blunt   nostalgic

Then write two sentences explaining your choice of words.

12 How can you tell that one story was written more recently than the other? What clues are there in the words and sentences? Write a brief paragraph explaining what you can tell about when they were written.

13 Study the similarities and differences in the two texts. Think about:

   ◆ the way the two narrators tell the stories

   ◆ the way the writers build suspense

   ◆ the disturbing mood of the texts.

Write two brief paragraphs explaining the similarities and differences. Then say which story you prefer and why.

LANGUAGE AND STRUCTURE

Text A

   1 The writer uses personification in his story, like this:

   Death, in approaching him, had stalked with his black shadow before him ...

   a What impression does this create of Death?

   b Why do you think the writer uses this technique?

   2 Sometimes the writer uses repetition to create an effect – for example:

   But the beating grew louder, louder!

   He might have said: 'But the beating grew louder and louder!' What effect do you think his use of repetition creates in this example?

Text B

3 Look at the writer's use of description. In the first sentence, what do you notice about the way he describes the wind?

4 Look at the way the young soldier speaks. How can you tell that:

a he is being polite?

b he feels nervous about the mission?

5 Now look at the narrator's speech. How can you tell that he is:

a blunt in his speech?

b sarcastic?

6 The writer includes speech within longer sentences that give more information about the speaker, or what he is thinking. Give an example of the writer integrating speech in this way.

WRITING ACTIVITY

Both writers help us to see into the minds of their narrators by using the first person ('I ...' rather than 'he ...').

How would the effect of the stories be different if they were written in the third person?

Choose one short extract from either story. Then rewrite it using the third person. Next, write a brief paragraph saying how you think the change of narrative voice changes the effect of the story.

Extended Writing

Choose one of the writers below. They are all listed in the national curriculum for English because they are influential in the history of English literature.

Playwrights:

William Congreve, Oliver Goldsmith, Christopher Marlowe, Sean O'Casey, Harold Pinter, J. B. Priestley, Peter Shaffer, G. B. Shaw, R. B. Sheridan, Oscar Wilde.

Fiction writers:

Jane Austen, Charlotte Brontë, Emily Brontë, John Bunyan, Wilkie Collins, Joseph Conrad, Daniel Defoe, Charles Dickens, Arthur Conan Doyle, George Eliot, Henry Fielding, Elizabeth Gaskell, Thomas Hardy, Henry James, Mary Shelley, Robert Louis Stevenson, Jonathan Swift, Anthony Trollope, H. G. Wells.

Poets:

Matthew Arnold, Elizabeth Barrett Browning, William Blake, Emily Brontë, Robert Browning, Robert Burns, Lord Byron, Geoffrey Chaucer, John Clare, S. T. Coleridge, John Donne, John Dryden, Thomas Gray, George Herbert, Robert Herrick, Gerard Manley Hopkins, John Keats, Andrew Marvell, John Milton, Alexander Pope, Christina Rossetti, William Shakespeare (sonnets), Percy Bysshe Shelley, Edmund Spenser, Alfred Lord Tennyson, Henry Vaughan, William Wordsworth, Sir Thomas Wyatt.

Assignment

Find out more about the writer you have chosen, and aim to produce a website or poster about that author, which includes:

◆ biographical information (the writer's background)

◆ titles of some texts that she or he has written

◆ an extract from one text to show the writer's style

◆ a comment about why the writer was so influential.

Your aim is to make the information about the writer interesting to a general audience. Assume that your readers do not know anything about the writer you have chosen. How will you make them want to start reading something by her or him?

On one side of A4 paper, sketch out how your webpage or poster might look. It should combine:

◆ images

◆ text

◆ some interactive features – e.g. a quiz or competition.

Think about the style of writing you will use to interest your reader: how formal or informal will you be? Will you use a serious or humorous tone?

To do your research you could use:

◆ the school library

◆ CD-roms of literary material (e.g. guides to writers, images, etc.)

◆ the Internet

Once you have finished your design, show it to other people in your group. Produce a class display on influential writers or – better still – create part of your school website devoted to this.

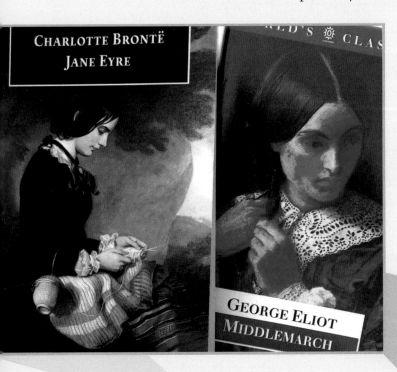

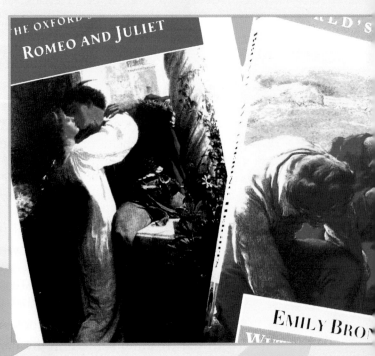

Influences on language and style

Introduction

Shakespeare is certainly the best-known dramatist in English. But many other playwrights have also been influential in the history of world literature. This unit focuses on a Norwegian writer who has been called 'the father of modern drama'.

When Henrik Ibsen's plays first appeared in the late nineteenth century, audiences across Europe were shocked and scandalized. So much so, in fact, that Ibsen had to leave his home at one point.

He was controversial for two reasons. First, his plays dealt with issues that few writers had had the courage to address. For example, he showed women stifled by society and in relationships, and treated as inferior. He showed what happened when they struggled to break free in a play called *A Doll's House*.

He was also controversial because of the way he used language. To audiences of the day, his language was shockingly ordinary. It was not literary language, it was like the language people really spoke in their daily lives. This was a new concept – and it is hard to imagine now how upset people became when they heard major issues spoken about in everyday words.

In this way, Ibsen paved the way for twentieth-century realism – showing life as it is – and for soap operas.

This unit allows you to compare two versions of Ibsen's writing. One is a translation of his play by Michael Meyer – famous for his Ibsen translations. The second is by the well-known American dramatist Arthur Miller. He wrote his own translation of Ibsen's play, and it enables you to compare two very different versions.

The play, called *An Enemy of the People*, is about Dr Thomas Stockmann, who learns that the water in his town's water supply is polluted. He knows he has to warn the people. But he quickly finds that this is less easy than he thinks – local politicians and the media are terrified of the effect of bad publicity. So they fight to stop him from making the truth known.

Start by reading the opening from Michael Meyer's translation of the play. Then compare it with Arthur Miller's. This extract takes place in Dr Stockmann's home and features his relatives, although he doesn't appear until later in the play.

Read the play aloud in a small group. For each script you will need readers for the following characters:

- Mrs Stockmann
- Billing
- Mayor (Peter Stockmann)
- Hovstad
- Morten Kiil (only in text B)

An Enemy of the People

Objectives

You will be studying the following objectives:

- Word level: *layers of meaning*
- Sentence level: *attitudes to Standard English*, and *trends over time*
- Reading: *authorial perspective, compare texts, rhetorical devices, analyse scenes, major writers*, and *different cultural contexts*
- Writing: *cite textual evidence*

Text A

Evening in DR STOCKMANN'S living-room. It is humbly but neatly furnished and decorated. In the wall to the right are two doors, of which the further leads out to the hall and the nearer to the DOCTOR'S study. In the opposite wall, facing the hall door, is a door that leads to the other rooms occupied by the family. In the middle of this wall stands a tiled stove; further downstage is a sofa with a mirror above it. In front of the sofa is an oval table

with a cloth on it. Upon this table stands a lighted lamp with a shade. Upstage, an open door to the dining-room in which can be seen a table laid for the evening meal, with a lamp on it.

At this table BILLING is seated, a napkin tucked beneath his chin. MRS STOCKMANN is standing by the table, offering him a plate with a large joint of beef on it. The other places around the table are empty, and the table is in the disorder of a meal that has been finished.

MRS STOCKMANN: There, Mr Billing! But if you will come an hour late, you'll have to put up with cold.

BILLING (*eating*): Oh, but this is capital. Absolutely capital!

MRS STOCKMANN: Well you know how punctually my husband always likes to eat –

BILLING: It doesn't bother me. I enjoy eating alone, without having to talk to anyone.

MRS STOCKMANN: Oh. Well, as long as you're enjoying it, that's – (*Listens towards the hall.*) Ah, this must be Mr Hovstad.

BILLING: Very likely.

MAYOR PETER STOCKMANN enters wearing an overcoat and his official hat and carrying a stick.

MAYOR: Good evening to you, my dear sister-in-law.

MRS STOCKMANN (*goes into the living-room*): Why, good evening! Fancy seeing you here! How nice of you to come and call on us!

MAYOR: I just happened to be passing so – (*Glances towards the dining-room.*) But I hear you have company.

MRS STOCKMANN (*a little embarrassed*): Oh, no, no, that's no one. (*Quickly.*) Won't you have something too?

MAYOR: I? No, thank you! Good heavens, a cooked meal at night! My digestion would never stand that!

MRS STOCKMANN: Oh, but surely just for once –

MAYOR: No, no! It's very kind of you, but I'll stick to my tea and sandwiches. It's healthier in the long run; and a little less expensive.

MRS STOCKMANN (*smiles*): You speak as though Thomas and I were spend-thrifts!

MAYOR: Not you, my dear sister-in-law. Such a thought was far from my mind. (*Points towards the DOCTOR'S study.*) Isn't he at home?

MRS STOCKMANN: No, he's gone for a little walk with the boys.

MAYOR: I wonder if that's wise so soon after a meal? (*Listens.*) Ah, this must be he.

MRS STOCKMANN: No, I don't think it can be, yet. (*A knock on the door.*) Come in!

HOVSTAD, the editor of the local newspaper, enters from the hall.

HOVSTAD: Yes. Please excuse me, I was detained down at the printer's. Good evening, Your Worship.

MAYOR (*greets him somewhat stiffly*): Good evening. I suppose you are here on business?

Trans. Michael Meyer

Text B

It is evening. Dr Stockmann's living room is simply but cheerfully furnished. A doorway, upstage right, leads into the entrance hall, which extends from the front door to the dining room, running unseen behind the living room. At the left is another door, which leads to the Doctor's study and other rooms. In the upstage left corner is a stove. Toward the left foreground is a sofa with a table behind it. In the right foreground are two chairs, a small table between them, on which stand a lamp and a bowl of apples. At the back, to the left, an open doorway leads to the dining room, part of which is seen. The windows are in the right wall, a bench in front of them.

As the curtain rises, Billing and Morten Kiil are eating in the dining room. Billing is junior editor of the People's Daily Messenger. *Kiil is a slovenly old man who is feeding himself in a great hurry. He gulps his last bite and comes into the living room, where he puts on his coat and ratty fur hat. Billing comes in to help him.*

BILLING: You sure eat fast, Mr Kiil. (*Billing is an enthusiast to the point of foolishness.*)

KIIL: Eating don't get you anywhere, boy. Tell my daughter I went home.

Kiil starts across to the front door. Billing returns to his food in the dining room. Kiil halts at the bowl of apples; he takes one, tastes it, likes it, takes another and puts it in his pocket, then continues on toward the door. Again he stops, returns, and takes another apple for his pocket. Then he sees a tobacco can on the table. He covers his action from Billing's possible glance, opens the can, smells it, pours some into his side pocket. He is just closing the can when Catherine Stockmann enters from the dining room.

MRS STOCKMANN: Father! You're not going, are you?

KIIL: Got business to tend to.

MRS STOCKMANN: Oh, you're only going back to your room and you know it. Stay! Mr Billing's here, and Hovstad's coming. It'll be interesting for you.

KIIL: Got all kinds of business. The only reason I came over was the butcher told me you bought roast beef today. Very tasty, dear.

MRS STOCKMANN: Why don't you wait for Tom? He only went for a little walk.

KIIL (*taking out his pipe*): You think he'd mind if I filled my pipe?

MRS STOCKMANN: No, go ahead. And here – take some apples. You should always have fruit in your room.

KIIL: No, no, wouldn't think of it.

The doorbell rings.

MRS STOCKMANN: That must be Hovstad. (*She goes to the door and opens it.*)

Peter Stockmann, the Mayor, enters. He is a bachelor, nearing sixty. He has always been one of those men who make it their life work to stand in the centre of the ship to keep it from overturning. He probably envies the family life and warmth of this house, but when he comes he never wants to admit he came and often sits with his coat on.

MRS STOCKMANN: Peter! Well, this is a surprise!

PETER STOCKMANN: I was passing by … (*He sees Kiil and smiles, amused.*) Mr Kiil!

KIIL (*sarcastically*): Your Honor! (*He bites into his apple and exits.*)

MRS STOCKMANN: You mustn't mind him, Peter, he's getting terribly old. Would you like a bite to eat?

PETER STOCKMANN: No, no thanks. (*He sees Billing now, and Billing nods to him from the dining room.*)

MRS STOCKMANN (*embarrassed*): He just happened to drop in.

PETER STOCKMANN: That's all right. I can't take hot food in the evening. Not with my stomach.

MRS STOCKMANN: Can't I ever get you to eat anything in this house?

PETER STOCKMANN: Bless you, I stick to my tea and toast. Much healthier and more economical.

MRS STOCKMANN (*smiling*): You sound as though Tom and I throw money out the window.

PETER STOCKMANN: Not you, Catherine. He wouldn't be home, would he?

MRS STOCKMANN: He went for a little walk with the boys.

PETER STOCKMANN: You don't think that's dangerous, right after dinner? (*There is a loud knocking on the front door.*) That sounds like my brother.

MRS STOCKMANN: I doubt it, so soon. Come in, please.

Hovstad enters. He is in his early thirties, a graduate of the peasantry struggling with a terrible conflict. For while he hates authority and wealth, he cannot bring himself to cast off a certain desire to partake of them. Perhaps he is dangerous because he wants more than anything to belong, and in a radical that is a withering wish, not easily to be borne.

MRS STOCKMANN: Mr Hovstad –

HOVSTAD: Sorry I'm late. I was held up at the printing shop. *(Surprised)* Good evening, Your Honor.

PETER STOCKMANN *(rather stiffly)*: Hovstad. On business, no doubt.

Trans. Arthur Miller

UNDERSTANDING THE TEXT

Text A

1 Write down one detail from the opening stage directions that tells you the play is set in the past.

2 Explain in your own words what the writer means by 'the table is in the disorder of a meal that had been finished'.

3 Why does Mr Billing enjoy eating alone?

Text B

4 Write down two ways in which the setting in this version of the play is different from text A.

5 What impression do you get from the description 'a ratty fur hat'?

6 How can you tell that Peter Stockmann is a fussy person?

7 What clues can you find in the language that:

   a Text A translates a text written a long time ago?

   b Text B is by an American writer?

8 Does the character of Peter Stockmann seem exactly the same in both texts, or do the two writers present him slightly differently? Support your response with examples.

9 Look at this comment on the two versions of the play:

Text A is less descriptive. It gives us the words that characters say, but little else. The stage directions in text B help us much more to visualize the scene.

Do you agree with this comment? Say why or why not.

10 Henrik Ibsen is described as a very modern writer because of the way he presents themes and characters, and his use of language. Write a paragraph giving your response to these two extracts.

   ♦ In what ways does he seem like a modern writer to you?

   ♦ Which of the two translations do you prefer and why?

LANGUAGE AND STRUCTURE

Text A

1 Look at the stage directions. Why do you think these are written in the present rather than the past tense?

2 In his first speech, Mr Billing says ' … this is capital. Absolutely capital!' This word was used in the past to describe something that was really good. Think of a word someone might use today in an informal situation.

3 What do we learn about Mrs Stockmann's character from this scene? Write down three things we are shown about her.

Text B

4 This version uses some non-standard language – for example:

Eating don't get you anywhere, boy.

   a How would this be expressed in standard English?

   b Why do you think the translator uses a non-standard form like this?

   c Why might plays use non-standard English more than some other types of text?

5 Look at the way Peter Stockmann is described in this text:

He has always been one of those men who make it their life work to stand in the centre of the ship to keep it from overturning.

   a What do you think the writer means by this metaphor?

   b Why do you think he uses a metaphorical phrase rather than a literal one?

6 This scene is structured around the entrances of characters.

   a Write down the order in which the characters appear onstage.

   b Does anyone exit the stage in this scene?

WRITING ACTIVITY

Plays rely on dialogue to tell their stories. Henrik Ibsen is famous for creating a new, realistic kind of dialogue.

a Choose one example from each text of dialogue that feels very authentic (just like real life).

Write each example down, then explain why it seems so realistic. Be as specific as you can about the words and phrases in your chosen pieces.

b Find one example from *either* of the texts where you think the dialogue seems less realistic. Write it down and explain why.

UNIT 16

EXTENDED WRITING

Henrik Ibsen is sometimes described as the writer who made soap opera possible.

In pairs of a small group, do a research project into soap operas. This will test your teamwork and problem-solving skills.

Try to answer this question:

Which soap opera uses language in the most realistic way?

Your task is to:

♦ compare two or more soap operas (e.g. *EastEnders* and *Coronation Street*)

♦ study the way they use language

♦ write a brief report giving your results, or make a presentation to your class.

First you should think about the following questions:

♦ What makes dialogue realistic?

♦ What features of everyday speech will you be looking for?

To help with these questions, you could listen to a conversation between two people in real life and note the features of language they use (e.g. repetition, not completing sentences, fillers like *er* and *um*, overlapping speech, no clear structure). Make a checklist of features.

Use this checklist when you listen to a one- or two-minute extract from two different soap operas. Ideally, you need to record these so that you can replay them for better analysis.

Once you have some results, think about how you will write them down and present your report. Remember that you are aiming to present information as clearly as possible to your audience. What layout features might help (e.g. tables, charts, bullet points)?

Poetic fable

Introduction

Literature in English has been influenced by texts from all kinds of cultures. Greek myths, for example, have played a powerful part in storytelling. Irish short stories, American drama, West Indian poetry, and European plays have all shaped the way English literature has developed.

This unit takes a poem from India and explores how far it feels like the kind of fable or legend we expect from early English literature.

Start by looking at the title and making some predictions – not just on what the poem will be about, but also the kind of poem it will be. Does the title remind you of other texts, in particular stories from your childhood?

Read the poem and look at the way the writer uses poetic language to unfold a story.

The Tiger and the Deer

OBJECTIVES

You will be studying the following objectives:

- Word level: *layers of meaning*
- Reading: *authorial perspective*, *rhetorical devices*, and *different cultural contexts*
- Writing: *narrative techniques*

GLOSSARY

lest – *in case*

THE TIGER AND THE DEER

Brilliant, crouching, slouching, what crept through the green
    heart of the forest,
Gleaming eyes and mighty chest and soft soundless paws of
    grandeur and murder?
The wind slipped through the leaves as if afraid lest its voice
    and the noise of its steps disturb the pitiless Splendour,
Hardly daring to breathe. But the great beast crouched and
    crept, and crept and crouched a last time, noiseless, fatal,
Till suddenly death leaped on the beautiful wild deer as it
    drank
Unsuspecting from the great pool in the forest's coolness and
    shadow,
And it fell and, torn, died remembering its mate left sole in the
    deep woodland, –-
Destroyed, the mild harmless beauty by the strong cruel
    beauty in Nature.
But the day may yet come when the tiger crouches and leaps no
    more in the dangerous heart of the forest,
As the mammoth shakes no more the plains of Asia;
Still then shall the beautiful wild deer drink from the coolness
    of great pools in the leaves' shadow.
The mighty perish in their might;
The slain survive the slayer.

Aurobindo Ghose

UNDERSTANDING THE TEXT

1 The poem describes two creatures. Find a word or phrase
which is used to describe the tiger and another word or
phrase which describes the deer.

2 What happens to the deer?

3 The writer mentions the 'heart of the forest' twice. Which two
adjectives are used to describe it?

4 How would you sum up what happens in the poem in one
sentence?

INTERPRETING THE TEXT

5 How does the writer show the power and danger of the tiger?

6 Why does the writer compare the tiger with the mammoth?

7 The poem is like a fable or a parable – a story with a message. What message do you think the poem is offering?

8 What is the writer's attitude to the two creatures: does he admire one more than the other, admire both equally, or remain neutral? Explain your answer.

LANGUAGE AND STRUCTURE

1 Look at the first four lines of the poem. How does the writer use patterns of words to show:

a the movement of the tiger?

b the silence?

2 The writer uses personification to describe the wind – treats it as if it is human. What does he show the wind to be like?

3 Find an example of the way the writer uses repetition of sounds or structures to create his effects. Write down the example, and then write a sentence describing how it works.

4 Part of the poem is written in the past tense. Part of it is written in the future tense. Find the line where the poem shifts to the future tense. Why do you think the writer does this?

WRITING ACTIVITY

How could the poem be retold in prose as a story for young children? Write a short story called 'The Tiger and the Deer' based on the poem, aimed at children aged 5 to 8.

Think about the narrative techniques you will use. Instead of using third-person narration, you could write from the point of view of the tiger, of the deer, or switch between both (multiple narration).

Extended Writing

In your English lessons you will be able to read drama, fiction and poetry by major writers from different cultures and traditions.

Here are some of the examples given in the national curriculum:

Drama: Athol Fugard, Arthur Miller, Wole Soyinka, Tennessee Williams.

Fiction: Chinua Achebe, Maya Angelou, Willa Cather, Anita Desai, Nadine Gordimer, Ernest Hemingway, H. H. Richardson, Doris Lessing, R. K. Narayan, John Steinbeck, Ngugi wa Thiong'o.

Poetry: E. K. Brathwaite, Emily Dickinson, Robert Frost, Robert Lowell, Les Murray, Rabindranath Tagore, Derek Walcott.

Choose one of these writers – perhaps one you know nothing about. Working on your own or in a pair, find out more about the writer. Research some details about the writer's background, and what she or he has written.

When you have collected your information, think about how you can present it most effectively to others in your class. Perhaps you can create a poster or display. Include the following:

- information on the writer's background
- titles of some texts by the writer
- an extract from a text to show the writer's style
- a comment on the way the writer reflects his or her culture.